With Love from

Roman Lives

O Roma nobilis, orbis et domina,
Cunctarum urbium excellentissima,
Roseo martyrum sanguine rubea,
Albis et vriginum liliis candida,
Salutem dicimus tibi per omnia.
Te benedicimus: salve per saecula.

O noble Rome, mistress of the world,
Most excellent of all cities,
Stained red with the red blood of martyrs,
Decorated white with the white lilies of virgins,
For all we salute you.
To you we give blessing: Hail for all ages.

– Anonymous
9th century AD

Roman Lives

by

Dorothy Harrer

Printed with support from the Waldorf Curriculum Fund

Published by:
Waldorf Publications at the
Research Institute for Waldorf Education
38 Main Street
Chatham, New York 12037

Title: *Roman Lives*
Author: Dorothy Harrer
Editor/proofreader: Meg Gorman
Layout/design: Ann Erwin
Images: Wikipedia Commons
ISBN #978-1-936367-70-2

Contents

Here, then, we have the civilization of personality.
Now is the time when man evolves personality,
under the influence of the Roman culture
that is spread abroad over the lands of the West.
With Rome begins the period to which man today
may still feel himself related. Present day mankind
is built up upon the personality of the individual.

– Rudolf Steiner
"On the Meaning of Life"
Copenhagen, May 23, 1912

Aeneas

The story loved by Alexander the Great was *The Iliad*, a long song or poem first recited by Homer and passed on by word of mouth. In later times it was written down so that we can read it today. Another such story was passed down by word of mouth among the people and, as it was the story of the founding of Rome, it was later written down by Virgil, a Roman poet. We know it today as Virgil's *Aeneid*. It is the story of Aeneas, the son-in-law of Priam, King of Troy. King Priam had a fair daughter, Creusa, who was married to Prince Aeneas, the son of Venus (Aphrodite) and a mortal man, Anchises. It was the will of the gods that Troy should be destroyed even though it was a holy city, "Holy Ilium." The gods took part in the war, and among the heroes were many who were the sons of gods or goddesses.

There is a story of an encounter, in battle, between Aeneas and Achilles, a Greek hero, the son of Peleus and Thetis. In the course of the battle on the plain surrounding the walls of Troy, Achilles came forth in search of Hector, Priam's noble son. The god Apollo stood by Aeneas and urged him to do battle with Achilles, saying, "Thou too art the son of a goddess, and thy mother is greater than his who is but a daughter of the sea. Drive straight at him with thy spear and let not his threats frighten thee."

Then Aeneas stood forth and faced Achilles who said, "Fightest thou with me because thou hopest to reign over the men of Troy? Thou wilt not find it easy."

Aeneas answered, "Think not to terrify me with words, son of Peleus, for I too am the son of a goddess. Let us make trial of one another."

Aeneas cast his spear. It struck Achilles' shield with a dreadful sound but did not pierce it through. Then Achilles cast his spear, which pierced through the shield of Aeneas but did not wound him. Achilles drew his sword and rushed upon Aeneas. Aeneas caught up a great stone to hurl at Achilles. As Achilles closed in on Aeneas, the gods took a hand in the outcome of the battle for it was not their will that Aeneas should die.

Neptune (Poseidon), the god of the sea, lifted up Aeneas and bore him above the ranks of men in battle; but first he drew Achilles' spear from the shield of Aeneas and laid it at Achilles' feet.

Achilles cried out in amazement, "This is a great wonder I see! My spear lies before me, but the man whom I sought to slay I see not. Of a truth, Aeneas is dear to the immortal gods."

When the Greeks entered Troy, and were burning it and killing the Trojans, Prince Aeneas was asleep in his palace unaware of the defeat. Hector's shade (ghost) appeared to him in a dream and warned him to flee with his family to a distant land. In the midst of his dream, Aeneas was awakened by the sounds of battle. He leaped up, seized his sword and spear and, rushing through the King's palace, he found old Priam in full armor preparing to enter the battle himself. Just then, the son of Achilles sprang upon the King and killed him.

Aeneas fought his way through the enemy heroes to try to save his own father, Anchises, and Creusa, his wife, and his little son, Iulus. In an empty hall he came upon Helen, the cause of all the bloodshed. In a rage, he was about to kill her when Venus appeared and stayed his hands, saying, "Remember, the gods themselves have long ago decreed that Troy should fall. Helen was chosen as the earthly reason for the Greeks to come against the Trojans." Then Venus opened Aeneas' eyes to see beyond the physical world, and he beheld Poseidon, Hera, and even Zeus, fighting and crushing the walls of Troy with their heavy blows. Then Venus entreated her son to flee from Troy to a different land. He remembered his dream of Hector's shade and so was persuaded.

He found his old father, Anchises, but it was not so easy to persuade him. The old man wanted to die fighting but saw Aeneas' little son playing on the palace floor as if nothing were happening. Above the child's head a bright flame was hovering. This was an omen to Anchises that he must follow Aeneas and that their descendants would endure in another land.

So they set forth, Aeneas leading Iulus and carrying Anchises on his back. Creusa followed behind. Once outside of Troy, Aeneas saw that many were following him but that his wife was missing. In great haste he went back the way he had come in search of her, but on the way her shade [ghost]

Aeneas Fleeing from Troy, Pompeo Batoni, Sabauda Gallery, Turin, Italy, 1753

appeared to him, for she had been killed. With great solemnity she begged him to go to the west where, on the banks of a river named Tiber, he would find a beautiful young bride who would comfort him.

Thus it was that Aeneas and his followers sailed away from Troy in many ships, in search of a new homeland. They sailed to the west till they came to one of the Aegean islands, the Isle of Delos. There they landed and went to a temple of Apollo and consulted the oracle as to where they should go. The oracle told them to seek the land in the west from whence their ancestors had come.

Aeneas did not know where this land was until one night he had a vision. One of his household gods appeared and bid him seek the land of Hesperia. Aeneas told Anchises about his vision, and Anchises remembered a forgotten prophecy that his descendants would find a home there from where their first ancestor, Dardanus, had come to Troy.

So they sailed ever westward and had as many adventures and troubles as Odysseus. They sailed past the land of the Cyclopes and rescued one of Odysseus' sailors, who had been left behind, from under the nose of Polyphemus himself who had come down to the shore. The Trojans rowed away from him in all haste. They rowed around a big island, Sicily, to avoid Scylla and Charybdis. They suffered a great windstorm which Hera (Juno) persuaded Aeolus to let loose, and they lost all but seven ships when Poseidon (Neptune) sent the wind away and calmed the seas.

They spent a year at the court of Queen Dido in her beautiful city of Carthage. Dido would have Aeneas stay with her to rule as king of Carthage. Aeneas was almost persuaded, but was reminded in a dream sent from Venus that his destiny lay elsewhere. His departure infuriated Dido, who sought revenge in Aeneas' destruction, but her efforts proved fruitless. At last, after many more adventures, during which time old Anchises died, Aeneas sailed northward and came in sight of the shores of Hesperia, or Italy.

It was one year since Anchises had died, and he appeared to Aeneas and bade him go to Cumae, a city which had been settled by Greeks, to consult the oracle of that place who lived in a cave by the seashore. The priestess was called the Sibyl. The Cumaean Sibyl was an ancient crone, the greatest prophetess in Italy. Through her the voices of the gods spoke their messages and prophecies. Anchises told Aeneas to ask her to lead him into the world where those who had died mingled with those who sought to be born on earth. There, said Anchises, he would be able to talk more at length with Aeneas and give him more details as to what he should do and where he should settle.

When Aeneas went to the Sibyl and asked her to guide him into Hades, she said she would do so as soon as he brought her a certain golden twig that was growing on a tree in a dark forest. Aeneas prayed for help, and Venus, his mother, sent two snow-white doves to lead him to the tree where he found the twig.

Once he gave the Sibyl the golden twig, she willingly led him to Hades. He met his father who told him just where to go and what to do next. At the same time, Anchises pointed out, among the unborn souls who were there awaiting the time of their birth on earth again, certain ones who were to be the descendants of Aeneas in future times. He told Aeneas what each one would achieve in life and he called them by name: Romulus, Camillus, Tiberius, Caius Gracchus, Julius Caesar and others. When the Sibyl led him back to the world, Aeneas knew what signs to follow.

As they sailed along the coast, they found the mouth of the River Tiber. Here they landed, took their household gods ashore and prepared to sacrifice a white sow, but she broke away and fled from the priests. Aeneas followed her, for Anchises had told him that a four-footed beast would lead him to the spot where he was to build a city. The sow ran ahead until she came to a hill about two miles from the shore. There she lay down and thirty young pigs were born. Aeneas looked at the land and saw that it was sandy and barren, and he doubted what he should do. Just then he heard a voice say, "The thirty young pigs are thirty years. When thirty years have passed, thy children will leave this place for a better land. Meantime, do thou obey the gods and build thy city on this place where they bid thee to build." Thus the Trojans built their city there.

This land belonged to a people who were farmers. Their king was Latinus; he was friendly to the Trojans and gave them land. But soon the Trojans quarreled with the people of the country and the quarrel developed into a war which Aeneas won. He then married the daughter of Latinus. Her name was Lavinia. Together with Latinus he ruled the country. The people came to be called "the Latins" and the country, "Latium." When Aeneas died, the people built an altar to him and worshipped him as a god by the name of Jupiter Indiges, meaning "the god who was of that very land."

After thirty years had passed, Iulus, the son of Aeneas, built a city on the slope of a high mountain above a lake. It was a long, narrow city because it was on such a steep slope. He named it Alba Longa, meaning the Long White City, "white" because of the omen of the white sow.

For three hundred years, eleven kings ruled over Alba Longa. The last of these kings was Procas. When he died, his two sons, Numitor and Amulius, became enemies. Amulius overcame Numitor and took the throne from him. To prevent Numitor's children from getting it back, he had the son killed and sent his daughter to a temple to become a priestess; but Mars, the god of war, fell in love with the priestess and gave her two sons who were to struggle with each other for the land founded by Aeneas.

LINES FROM VIRGIL'S *AENEID*

Arma virumque cano, Troiae qui primus ab oris
Italiam fato profugus Lavinaque venit
Litora, multum ille et terris iactatus et alto
Vi superum, saevae memorem Iunonis ob iram,
Multa quoque et bello passus, dum conderet urbem
Inferretque deos Latio, genus unde Latinum
Albanique patres atque altae moenia Romae.

Arms and the man I sing, who first made way,
Predestined exile, from the Trojan shore
To Italy, the blest Lavinian strand.
Smitten of storms was he on land and sea
By violence of heaven, to satisfy
Stern Juno's sleepless wrath; and much in war
He suffered, seeking at the last to found
The city, and bring o'er his father's gods
To safe abode in Latium; whence arose
The Latin race, old Alba's reverend lords,
And from her hills wide-walled, imperial Rome.

– Translation by T.C. Williams

CREUSA'S FAREWELL TO AENEAS

Quid tantum insano iuvat indulgere dolori,
O dulcis coniunx? Non haec sine numine divom
Eveniunt nec te hinc comitem asportare Creusam
Fas, aut ille sinit superi regnator Olympi.
Longa tibi exsilia, et vastum maris aequor arandum:
Et terram Hesperiam venies, ubi Lydius arva
Interropima virum leni fluit agmine Thybris;
Illic res laetae regnumque et regia coniunx
Parta tibi; lacrimas dilectae pelle Creusae.
Tamque vale, et nati servo communis amorem.

Why to these frenzied sorrows bend thy soul,
O husband ever dear? The will of heaven
Hath brought all this to pass. Fate doth not send
Creusa the long journeys thou shalt take,
Nor hath the Olympian King so given decree.
Long is thy banishment; thy ship must plough
The vast, far-spreading sea. Then shalt thou come
Unto Hesperia, whose fruitful plains
Are watered by the Tiber, Lydian stream,
Of smooth, benignant flow. Thou shalt obtain
Fair fortunes, and a throne and royal bride.
For thy beloved Creusa weep no more.
Farewell! Farewell! O, cherish evermore thy son and mine.

– Translation by John Dryden

The Founding of Rome

(A compilation from plays written by Sixth Graders)

Characters:

Martius, Metellus	two soldiers
Romulus, Remus	grandsons of King Numitor
Marcellus	a fruit vendor
Marcus	his small son
Cassius	wine merchant
Servius, Publius	two shepherds

Scene: A roadway on the plain between the Aventine and Palatine Hills, where there is a spring or fountain. As the curtain opens, Martius and Metellus appear, from right and left, to meet each other at center stage.

Martius: Hail, Metellus! Did you not hear the news?

Metellus: No, tell me!

Martius: The two grandsons of Numitor have turned up!

Metellus: How did Numitor find them?

Martius: A shepherd's quarrel! The shepherds of Numitor caught one, Remus, grazing the flocks of Faustulus in Numitor's pastures on the Aventine slope. They brought him before their master. Then Faustulus himself appeared with Romulus, the twin of Remus, to plead forgiveness. Then did Numitor question Faustulus to find that the twins were none other than the sons of Rhea Sylvia, Numitor's daughter.

Metellus: What will come of this? 'Twas said that Amulius destroyed the babes without a qualm. Does he know of their survival?

Martius: Does he know! No sooner were the twins made familiar with their origin than they turned toward Alba Longa and without loss of any time made entrance before the throne where Amulius held court.

Metellus: How spoke they then? Have they been bound and chained to await their doom, or have they already met their mother's shade in Pluto's realm?

Martius: Amulius had time to rise but not to speak before the brothers called on him to die for his crime against their mother and therewith made an end of him. And when the deed was done, they claimed the throne again for Numitor.

(Voice heard offstage)

Romulus: Now that our grandfather, King Numitor, is back on the throne, he wants us to live with him in Alba Longa.

Martius: Here come the twins. Let us step aside and hear their argument.

(The two soldiers move back stage, center, beside the spring.)

(Enter Romulus and Remus.)

Romulus: I would rather build a city for myself and give it my name.

Remus: That's just what I would like to do, my brother.

Romulus: And it will be built on the Palatine Hill for we were raised there. The gods would sorely be offended if we did not build the city there.

Remus: Nay, brother Romulus, can you not see that we should build the city on the Aventine Hill. There the pastures are rich and green, and we may graze our flocks nearby and have good ground under our city.

Romulus: Go your way, brother. The Aventine lies there.

(Pointing to the left, Romulus exits right. Remus turns and exits left.)

Metellus: *(coming forward)* May the favor of the gods go with Remus. He has chosen wisely indeed. I shall follow him. *(Metellus exits to the left.)*

Martius: Nay, I shall follow Romulus. He is wise to remember the place of his raising. *(Exits right.)*

(Marcellus, the fruit vendor, enters from the right with his son, while Cassius, the wine merchant, enters from the left.)

Cassius: Greetings, old friend. What news is there since I last saw you?

Marcellus: Have you heard that Romulus and Remus, grandsons of the King, are going to build a new city?

Cassius: Nay, I have not. Where is the city to be?

Marcellus: Remus speaks for the Aventine Hill, but Romulus has chosen the Palatine Hill where they were brought up by the shepherd Faustulus.

Marcus: If they are grandsons of the King, why were they brought up by a shepherd?

Marcellus: Because they were found by Faustulus as babes—in a she-wolf's den near the edge of the River Tiber.

Marcus: Babies in a wolf's den?

Marcellus: 'Twas said that Amulius cast them into the flood waters because as grandsons of the rightful king they might grow up to take the throne. The she-wolf rescued them and cared for them until Faustulus found them and took them in.

Cassius: Both boys are leaders, at least they were among the shepherds of Faustulus. It will not be easy for one to give in to the other.

Marcellus: It is rumored that King Numitor hath bid them seek an omen from the heavens—to watch the flights of birds and the like, and so to let the gods decide their quarrel.

(Servius and Publius enter.)

Servius: There is Romulus, hero of the people.

(Romulus appears at right attended by Martius and others. They are scanning the skies.)

Publius: There comes Remus, soon to be our king.

(He points left as Remus appears attended by Metellus and others. They are also scanning the skies.)

Servius: The ways of the gods are strange. The twins have always been together and now, because only one can be King, they have taken their separate ways.

Publius: Aye, each to watch for a sign from the heavens, Remus from the Aventine Hill and Romulus on the Palatine.

Remus: *(running toward Romulus)* I have seen six vultures flying above the Aventine Hill. Thus have the gods given their sign to build the city there.

Romulus: Twelve vultures are circling the Palatine Hill!

(The people all run toward Romulus shouting.)

The People: For Romulus is the omen!

Romulus: *(wielding his shovel)* Here I start the wall to rise around my city. It will keep out all my enemies.

Remus: *(approaches and laughs)* It may keep an infant out, but your enemies will jump over it like this! *(He jumps over the invisible wall and laughs again.)*

(Romulus strikes Remus with his shovel and Remus falls. Metellus bends over him and touches him, then stands.)

Metellus: Thou hast slain thy brother. Remus is dead.

Romulus: Thus shall it be to any man who dares to pass over my walls.

CURTAIN

The Seven Kings of Rome

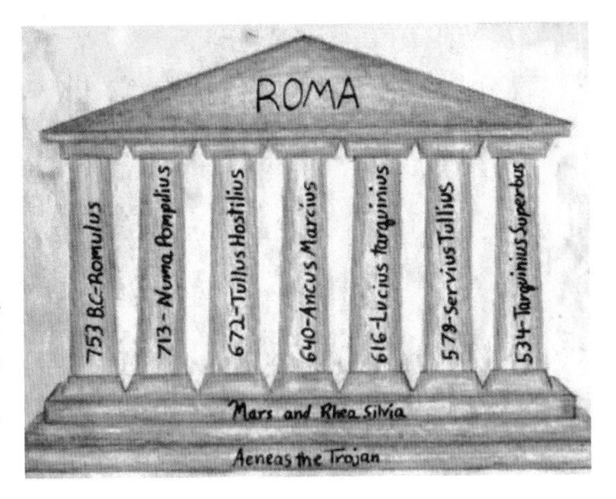

AMOR means LOVE
ROMA means POWER

On the 21st of April, in 753 BC, Romulus, the powerful, founded his city after he had slain his brother, Remus, and became sole ruler of the new kingdom. For the next 300 years Rome was ruled by kings, Romulus being the first of seven.

The history of this time was written down hundreds of years later from stories and legends that had been told by word-of-mouth. So it is called "a legendary time." Yet in these stories we have a true picture of the spirit of Rome, which was so different from the spirit of Greece.

What was happening in the rest of the world during these three centuries of the time of the Seven Kings?

» The Assyrians conquered the land between the two rivers, the Tigris and the Euphrates.
» The Hebrews were led into captivity in Babylon.
» Nineveh was conquered by the Persians, who also conquered King Croesus in Lydia as well as the land of Egypt, and the great Persian Empire was established.
» Solon became the law giver in Athens.
» Thales of Miletus foretold the sun's eclipse.
» Pythagoras founded his school.

At the time that Romulus ruled Rome, there was in Israel among the Jews, a prophet named Isaiah who foretold a great world event: "For unto us a son is born, unto us a son is given, and the government shall be upon his shoulders, and his name shall be called Wonderful, Counselor, the Mighty God, the Everlasting Father, the Prince of Peace." (Isaiah 9:6)

ROMULUS

Etruscan bronze statue of Romulus and Remus being suckled by a she-wolf, Capitoline Museum, Rome

Romulus was the son of Mars (Ares), the god of war. And it was the wolf, a beast of prey, who mothered him. After Rome was founded, it became a city of 3000 men who, as subjects of Romulus, were called Romans. All were armed, and there were no women. To enlarge the population, Romulus invited all kinds of fugitives to become citizens.

The wall that was built around the city of Rome was considered holy, but the gates were not. Within the walls the dwellings surrounded the Comitium, a center wherein the Romans assembled and where sanctuaries were preserved, such as the "lupercal" or sanctuary of the wolves; the "Vediovis" or sanctuary of Jupiter; a holy fig tree; the straw-covered house of Romulus (the shepherd's hut of Faustulus); and the "Mundus Cereris," a vault or pit which Romulus dug and in which were kept all the requisites of a household and a handful of beloved native earth. There was also the *curia saliorum,* the building containing the altars of each of the "curiae."

The 3000 Romans who were the first subjects of Romulus were divided into three tribes. Each tribe of 1000 was divided into 10 curiae of 100 men each. Each man represented a house and in time a family. As citizens the curiae met as the assembly, while the senate was made up of 200 senators chosen equally from the two higher tribes. Within the walls of Rome, each citizen had a right to appeal to the assembly should the King or his judges accuse him unjustly.

As more people became Romans, without belonging to the three tribes, thirty more tribes were established and classed according to the location of their property. They met in their own assemblies. Thus, two bodies existed alongside each other, the curiae regarding themselves as *the* Roman people and not allowing the others, called the "commons," to take part in the highest acts of national sovereignty. Only in times of war did they unite as one great body. A man's position in the army equaled his position in the state and depended on wealth and property. In the early days, the ruling class fought on horseback, fully armed. Their dependents fought on foot. Most of them could not supply themselves with complete armor. Only those in the foremost ranks needed to be fully armed. The thirty tribes of the commons paralleled the thirty curiae. There were three *centuries* (3 x 100) horsemen in each, which made six centuries when they united in war. Thus did Romulus and his followers shape Rome as a great military state.

Other tribes of people around Rome opposed the growth of the city. Among these tribes were the Sabines who invaded Rome and were not only conquered, but the Sabine women were captured and taken as wives to the Romans. Rome also conquered new lands in the region around the city and the conquered people came under the rule of Rome as free men but not as citizens. They were termed "plebeians" and not permitted to belong to the Roman tribes or curiae nor allowed a share in the government or property of the state. They could not intermarry with Roman families. Among those conquered were the Latins who were given the Aventine Hill on which to live. They were not admitted to live in Rome but were protected by the

Rape of the Sabine Women, Jacopo Ligozzi (1547–1627), oil on canvas, Detroit Institute of Arts, 1605

Romans against foreign enemies. For a long time to come, the plebeians were the foot soldiers and served under the Patricians, who descended from the "Fathers of the State."

As the first King, Romulus ruled over Rome for 38 years, until 715 BC. Through his deeds he seemed to paint a picture of the human being as a warrior who seeks power for himself and his country. The time came when the very men whom he had chosen to help him, the 200 senators, revolted against his tyranny and murdered him. They told the people that he had been lifted into heaven by the gods. The people began to murmur until one of the oldest senators, whose word they had always respected, came before them and announced that Romulus had appeared to him in more than mortal beauty and stature, and had said, "Go and tell my people that they should weep not for me anymore. But bid them to be brave and warlike, and so they shall make my city the greatest in the earth." Then the people were convinced that Romulus had become a god and offered sacrifices to him and worshipped him by the name of the god Quirinus.

NUMA POMPILIUS

Romulus had had no son, and for a year after his death, the Romans had no king. Rome now included the original Romans, who lived on the Palatine Hill, and the Sabines, who had been joined to the Romans but who lived on the Capitoline and Quirinal Hills. The senators took turns ruling Rome, ten men every five days, because they could not decide whether to choose a Roman or a Sabine as their new king. The people began to grumble and complain that they had no king to lead their armies in case of war with certain hostile tribes. At last it was decided that the next king should be a Sabine but that the Romans would choose him.

It happened that among the Sabines was a man named Numa Pompilius, who was as different from Romulus as day is from night. Numa Pompilius had lived a quiet and peaceful life, withdrawn from people, in an effort to grow in wisdom. He was known to be wise, just and pious. It was even said that he had been a student of Pythagoras, the great Greek mathematician and teacher. The Romans chose him to be their king, for perhaps they had sickened of the violence and bloodshed that surrounded the rule of Romulus.

Ein Augur erklärt Numa Pompilius nach dem Orakel des Vogelfluges zum König [An Augur Explains to Numa Pompilius after an Oracle of Birdflight that He Is to Be King], Bernard Rode (1725–1797), engraving, 1768

Ambassadors from Rome went to Numa's quiet, country home to ask him to be King, but, to their surprise, he did not accept at once. He had to be persuaded. His own kinsmen argued that he should accept, that it was his duty, saying, "It is God himself who now calls upon your wisdom." Then Numa agreed only on the condition that he would receive an augury from the gods themselves that it was their will for him to become King.

The Romans led him to Capitoline Hill, where a priest laid his hand on Numa's head and prayed that Jupiter (Zeus) would send a sign of his favor. Below and around the hill, all the people were waiting in silence and devotion. Even as they heard the prayer of the priest, they saw birds, which were to them always a sign of heaven's wishes, flying across the sky. At the omen of the birds, Numa allowed the royal robes to be laid upon his shoulders, and he went down from the hill to be welcomed by the cheering people as their King.

Romulus' spirit had bid his people be brave and warlike, but Numa Pompilius was a man of peace, and throughout his long reign he tried to show the people that peace, and not war, would make them great.

How did he do this? He built a temple to Janus who, it was told in legends, in very ancient times had been one of those gods who came to earth as a leader and king and who, like Osiris, had spent his life on earth teaching human beings not to be brutal and savage but to live helpfully with each other. The doors of this temple were to remain closed in times of peace when the people did not need the help of Janus. They were to be opened only in times of war, that people might pray for peace. Numa Pompilius reigned for 43 years and the doors of the temple remained closed the whole time, for Rome was at peace.

As guardian of the peace, Numa also strengthened the more invisible walls of peace: certain laws and customs to keep people at peace: He taught people that their prayers to the gods should be serious and unhurried. He named a man as chief priest, Pontifex Maximus, and placed under his authority the laws of worship and of the way in which priests were to be selected. He placed priestesses in the Temple of Vesta, the Goddess of the Hearth, and they were to see that the sacred fire of the city never died out. Thus, Numa Pompilius was the founder of organized religion in Rome.

He put certain men in positions, not as generals but as guardians of the peace. He had made a law that no men could take up arms against others until all hope of settling disputes through discussion was ended. The "guardians of the peace" were to prevent disputes, to put a stop to them before they could reach an end of discussion.

Numa believed that nothing made a man desire peace so much as a country life wherein he could cultivate his own fields, so he divided the land among the people to give each man his own field.

To keep peace between the Romans and the Sabines, who were apt to become jealous of each other and quarrelsome, he formed companies, not of soldiers but of musicians, goldsmiths, carpenters, dyers, shoemakers, skinners, brass workers, potters and so on. These companies, or guilds, were thus the meeting places of both Romans and Sabines who now thought of each other as fellow musicians, goldsmiths, and so forth.

It was not only the Romans who felt the mild and peace-loving spirit of Numa, but, throughout the neighboring lands and cities, it was as if a healthful and gentle air had blown from Rome upon them. They too began to live at peace, tilling the soil, bringing up their children and worshiping their gods. Instead of wars between the cities, there were friendly visits. Instead of celebrations of victory or mournings for defeat, there were festivals of planting and of harvest in which all shared. Numa's love of goodness and justice seemed to overflow and flood all of Italy as from a fountain, and his serene spirit spread its calm throughout the land.

Detail from *The Nymph Egeria Dictating Laws to Numa Pompilius,* painting by Ulpiano Checa (1860–1916)

Numa lived to be 80 years old, and he died of old age as gently and peacefully as he had lived. All the neighboring states sent their ambassadors to his funeral to do him honor.

Numa Pompilius ruled Rome between circa 714 to 671 BC. When he died, the senators again ruled for a time until they found a man whom they chose to be the third King of Rome.

TULLUS HOSTILIUS

Tullus Hostilius was chosen by the senators because he was a Roman and because his grandfather had fought with Romulus against the Sabines.

After Numa's death, the spirit of peace seemed to weaken. Friendly feelings between the Romans and the countrymen of Alba Longa in the hills outside of Rome gave way to quarreling because people began to raid each other's fields and gardens, stealing each other's crops and animals.

When the ruler of the Albans complained to Tullus Hostilius, he, like a small boy, took the attitude, "You started it!" The Alban and Roman armies prepared to fight. In the meantime, Tullus and the Alban King agreed that only picked men should engage in battle and that the winning side would take dominion over the other.

So it came about that the Albans sent three brothers from a family named Curiatius against three brothers of a Roman family named Horatius. Both families were descendants of Aeneas.

The three Curiatii were as brave as the three Horatii. As the Roman and Alban armies stood by to watch the contest, the six young warriors were filled with courage and devotion to their own people and never gave a thought to their common ancestor. As they struggled against each other, not one of them showed fear. In the contest the Albans killed two of the Romans, but in so doing all three Curiatii were wounded severely.

La victoire de Tullus Hostilius sur les forces de Veies et de Fidena [The Victory of Tullus Hostilius over the Forces of Veii and Fidenae], Giusette Cesari (1568–1640), Musée des Beaux-Arts de Caen, circa 1601

The remaining Horatius knew that he could not stand up to the three Curiatii, but he also knew they were wounded. He devised a plan to win the fight. He pretended to flee. Being wounded, each of his enemies went after him at different speeds. Thus he was able to meet them one by one. The Horatius slew them all. When the third brother of the Curiatii, wounded and exhausted and unable to defend himself, came upon Horatius, he stood before the Roman without lifting a weapon, and Horatius shouted, "Two have I sent to join the shades of my two brothers! The third I will offer to Rome that the Roman may rule the Alban." Then Horatius thrust his sword down the throat of the wounded man and stripped him of his armor and his cloak.

As the Romans led Horatius back to Rome in a triumphal procession, his sister, Horatia, came out to meet him. She saw that the cloak he carried was one that she had made and given to the one young Curiatius whom she had loved and promised to marry. She cried out in anguish. As her tears and sobs startled all who were cheering her brother's victory for Rome, he drew his sword and stabbed her to the heart, shouting, "So shall perish every Roman maiden who weeps for her country's enemy!"

Many men cried out against this dreadful deed. The young Horatius was then judged before all the Roman people. For two reasons, they did not condemn him: because he had conquered the enemies of Rome and because the father and sister of the Curiatius said that they considered Horatia lawfully slain.

According to the agreement between the Romans and the Albans, the Albans now became subjects of the Roman State; but when Tullus Hostilius called on them to help the Romans in another war, the Alban leader stayed out of the battle. Nevertheless, the Romans were victorious and Tullus sought revenge on the Albans and their leader.

He called the Albans together as if to address them. They were then surrounded by Roman soldiers in a close circle so that they could neither run nor fight. Then the Roman King had the Alban leader tied between two horse-drawn chariots, which were driven off in two directions. The Alban was torn in two. Tullus Hostilius sent the Roman army to Alba Longa, it destroyed the city completely. Then he ordered all the Albans to move to the Caelian Hill as Roman citizens.

Tullus Hostilius continued as a warring king. He engaged in another war with the Sabines. So busy was he with one war after another that he neglected any service to the gods. A dreadful plague came upon the Romans. Even Tullus was stricken with it. He begged Jupiter for his favor and help. The god's answer was a bolt of lightning, which shot down from heaven to burn the King and his house to ashes.

This was an omen to the Romans that they had better choose a new king who would follow the example of Numa Pompilius. They chose the grandson of Tullus Hostilius.

ANCUS MARTIUS

The new king straightway had Numa's religious and peaceful laws written out on white boards and posted throughout the city, and he decreed that people must observe them. Yet, the warlike feelings of the Romans and of the people in the surrounding kingdoms, feelings that had sprung up since Numa's death, led to one more conflict. The other Latin states attacked the Romans, but they were defeated. Ancus Martius gave them the Aventine Hill as an abode. Now Rome included:

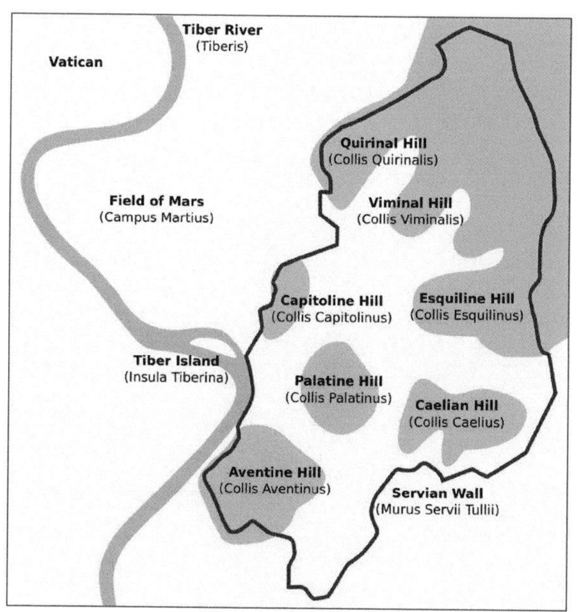

–the Palatine Hill inhabited by the original Romans,

–the Capitoline Hill of the Sabines,

–the Caelian Hill that had been given to the Albans,

–the Aventine Hill assigned to the Latins.

Then Ancus Martius took over the Janiculum Hill, across the River Tiber, to prevent possible new enemies from having it. From the Janiculum he built the first bridge across the Tiber, but only of wood so that it could be taken apart should enemies approach. His other achievement was to build Ostia, at the mouth of the Tiber, as a seaport for Rome.

During the reign of Ancus Martius, a stranger arrived in Rome. He was a Greek who had married the daughter of one of the leading families in Etruria, north of Rome. The Etruscans were skilled in the art of augury, or the reading of signs in nature. The stranger's name was Lucius Tarquinius and his wife's name was Tanaquil.

As their chariot reached the Janiculum in their approach to Rome, an eagle flew down from the heavens, gently hovered above Tarquinius, took the cap from Tarquinius' head, circled around the chariot uttering loud cries, then returned the cap. Tanaquil, knowing all signs of heavenly favors, told her husband that the eagle augured a great future for him in Rome.

Lucius Tarquinius became a friend of Ancus Martius who named Tarquinius to be the guardian of his children after his death. Ancus had ruled for 24 years when death came. His children were young, so the Romans chose Tarquinius as their King.

LUCIUS TARQUINIUS PRISCUS

Now the Romans had a king of Greek descent, but he was a patriotic Roman. His father, Demaratus, was a merchant from Corinth who had settled in Tarquinii in Etruria. He was treated as a stranger in Etruria and because of this, his son, having heard that strangers were welcome in Rome, had come to Rome. There he had first become a Roman citizen, then had shown such unusual abilities and devotion to the State that it was not hard for the Romans to choose him as their King. He became king in 616 BC and ruled for 38 years.

Tarquin and the Eagle, from *Story of the Romans* by Helen Gueber, 1896

During his reign there were three wars through which Rome conquered many neighboring cities. Tarquinius Priscus, however, was not just a conqueror. He was a builder. He had drains built between the hills to dry out the land. He sponsored the building of the Roman Forum as a marketplace and the Circus Maximus as a race course between the Palatine and Aventine Hills. He started the holding of contests or games in the Circus. He also built a new temple to the gods on the Capitoline Hill.

Wolfgang Sauber

Murder of Tarquinius Priscus, Sgraffito House, Lower Austria

Tarquinius had a slave named Servius Tullius. There was a mystery about his birth. Some said he was the son of a god. He served the King well and married the King's daughter. The sons of Ancus Martius, fearing that Tarquinius would make Servius his heir, plotted to kill Tarquinius and seize the throne. Thus it happened that two shepherds quarreled and called on the King to judge between them. As the King approached them, they attacked him, struck him down and fled. Tarquinius died but his wife pretended he had been only wounded. She announced that the King's will was for Servius Tullius to rule in his name until he should be well again. Servius then acted as king until people were accustomed to him; then when the death of Tarquinius Priscus was announced, they allowed Servius Tullius to become the king. The sons of Ancus Martius fled from Rome and spent the rest of their days in foreign lands.

SERVIUS TULLIUS

Servius Tullius was a just and good king. He loved the "commons," the poor people, and made laws to protect them from the rich. He conquered the Etruscans and gave them the Esquiline and Viminal Hills as their part of the city. He finished building a city wall, which Tarquinius had started, around all seven hills of Rome.

Ernst Wilhelm Hildebrand

Tullia in a Chariot in Front of the Capitol, photograph, 1885

He decreed that after him Rome should have no king, but that two men were to be chosen by the people to govern them year by year. He then made ready to give up the kingship.

Servius had two daughters. The older one was a gentle person, but the younger had a wicked heart. These two were married to Tarquinius' sons. The gentle girl married the proud and evil-hearted son whose name was Lucius. The wicked girl married Aruns, who was of a gentle nature. Evil could not bear to be joined to the good! Lucius slew his wife in secret, and Tullia, the younger sister, slew Aruns. Then the two evil souls married each other.

The Roman nobles hated Servius Tullius, and Lucius plotted with them to push him from the throne; they had him killed on his way home. Driving her chariot over her father's dead body, Tullia hailed Lucius Tarquinius Superbus as King of Rome. Servius had been Rome's ruler for 44 years.

LUCIUS TARQUINIUS SUPERBUS

Tarquinius Superbus gained his power wickedly and used it wickedly. He kept a guard of armed men around him and ruled all at his own will. He despised the senators, slew those who grumbled against him, and made no new senators to take their place. He canceled all the good laws of Servius and let the rich oppress the poor whom he used as slaves to dig drains and build temples. He was such a slave-master that many poor people took their own lives in misery. In the days of Superbus, it was often a happier thing to die than to live.

Though he paid little attention to the gods, Tarquin destroyed the old Sabine temples on Capitol Hill and built new ones. While digging, someone found a human skull and this was called a sign that Rome would be the *head* of all the earth. Signs? Omens? Auguries? Prophecies? These were looked for by the Romans of these early days.

Tarquinius Superbus, Lawrence Alma-Tadema (1836–1912), oil on panel, private collection, 1867

One day an ancient woman appeared before Tarquin. She bore nine great books which she offered to sell him for a price. The old woman was the Cumaean Sibyl, and she claimed that the books contained oracles and prophecies that would be of value to him. Finding the price too high, the King refused to buy the books. The Sibyl tossed three of the books into a fire and offered the remaining six for twice the price of the nine. Again Tarquin refused to buy, so the Sibyl tossed another three into the fire and again doubled the price of the last

Brutus Kissing the Earth, Giuseppe Crespi (1665–1747), National Museum in Warsaw, 1725

three. By this time, the King feared that he had not been acting wisely and bought the last three books at her price. He had them placed in a stone chest in a temple on the Capitol, and they were guarded by "the two men of the sacred books."

One day Tarquin saw a snake crawling from under the altar in his palace courtyard to devour the offerings on the altar. Not able to find out what this augured, he sent his two sons and their cousin to Delphi to consult the Oracle. The cousin's name was Brutus, meaning "dullard," because he had always seemed stupid. He was not stupid, really, but pretended to be because he was rich and feared Tarquin would kill him for his wealth.

Brutus took a gift to the Delphic Oracle. As a reference to himself, it was a hollow horn filled with gold, dull to look upon but a golden wit within. When the three had asked the Oracle the King's question and received the answer, they asked their own question, "O Lord Apollo, tell us which of us shall be the king in Rome?"

Then came a voice, "Whoever of you shall first kiss his mother."

The sons of Tarquin agreed to draw lots as to who should kiss their mother first when they would reach home. As they left the Temple, Brutus, pretended to stumble, fell down and kissed the earth, saying, "The earth is the true mother of us all."

Rome was at war when the three returned. The youngest son of Tarquin, who had not gone to Delphi, had just committed a crime. As a result, a noble lady had slain herself after calling upon her husband and Brutus to punish the whole family of Tarquins. Brutus led the people in the revolt and drove the Tarquins from Rome. This was the end of the rule of kings in Rome.

Then the people met on the Campus Martius and voted to return to the laws of Servius: to follow his will and elect two men every year to be their rulers. These men were to be called consuls and take turns every month as rulers of Rome. They elected Brutus and a man named Collatinus as their first consuls.

Tarquinius Superbus still plotted to regain his throne, and certain young Romans took part in this plot. Among them were the two sons of Brutus. A slave happened to overhear their talk and told the consuls all that he had heard. They had the boys seized and found letters to Tarquin on them.

Now a strange and piteous event took place. Brutus and Collatinus were sitting on their judgment seats in the Forum. Brutus' two sons were brought before them to be bound, scourged and beheaded. Brutus neither stirred from his seat nor looked away from the sight; yet men saw that his heart was grieving inwardly for his children. They marveled at him because he had loved justice more than his own blood.

Heroes of the Republic

Tarquinius Superbus was banished from Rome and the rule of kings came to its end in 510 BC. Now Rome became a republic under the rule of the consuls who, in time of danger and with senate approval, could appoint one man to be sole ruler for a limited time to lead the army and have complete power. He was called "Dictator." Otherwise, the consuls led the troops, controlled the treasury, and held the kingly powers while they were in office. They had to be at least 45 years old and to have had experience in other government offices. At first only patricians were elected as consuls, but by 367BC, plebeians could qualify as well.

When the Republic was established, Rome was a small nation ruling only the seven hills and little other land; it was surrounded on all sides by enemies. For 250 years she carried out wars with these enemies and gradually conquered them. By 264 BC she finally ruled all of Italy.

The stories of this time were written by Livy in his *History of Rome* which filled 142 books, 35 of which still exist. Livy was not yet born during the time of the Republic, but by gathering information as best he could, he wrote of heroes whose greatest aim was to do their duty to their city.

HORATIUS COCLES

Horatius Cocles, who had one blind eye, was a descendant of the Horiatius who slew the Curiatii. His heroism is described in the poem "Horatius at the Bridge" by Thomas B. MacCauley, in his *Lays of Ancient Rome*. This Horatius saved Rome from a defeat by the Etruscans.

The Etruscans had been a seafaring people who had landed along the coast of Italy in ages past and who had pushed inland and settled north of the Tiber. They were more civilized than the Latins and had traded with Greece. Lars Porsena, the King of Clusium, an Etrurian city, was persuaded by Tarquinius Superbus to help him regain his throne in Rome.

Horatius Cocles, Diana Scultori and Guilui Romano, 16th century Italy, Los Angeles County Museum of Art

The Etruscans first attacked the Romans on the Janiculum and drove them down and across the bridge over the Tiber. The young soldier, Horatius Cocles, with two other commanders, stopped at the entrance over the bridge, faced the enemy, and fought to keep the attackers back while the other Romans escaped over the bridge into Rome. Then Horatius sent the two commanders to ask the consuls to have the bridge cut off next to the Roman shore of the Tiber and to signal him when it was done by speaking more loudly. Then he stood alone upon the bridge as the enemy advanced. He struck some with his sword, beat others down with his shield, and kept back all who tried to cross the bridge. Only a few at a time could stand on the bridge, and the land there came to a point so that the river defended him at each side.

From a distance the enemy threw spears and darts at him. Horatius picked up the weapons thrown at him and hurled them back, easily hitting one or another because the Etruscans were crowded together. He suffered many wounds, the worst when a spear passed through his thigh. But then he heard the signal that the bridge was cut. So he leapt into the Tiber in full armor and with great difficulty swam through the swirling river safely to the other side. The Romans had been saved from immediate invasion, and Horatius was welcomed as a great hero. He was given lands, and a bronze statue of him was placed in the Forum. But he could never be a soldier again because of his lameness.

CAIUS MUCIUS

The Etruscans camped outside of Rome and kept food from going in. The Romans began to suffer hunger.

Caius Mucius was a young patrician. He went to the Senate and volunteered to go right into the Etruscan camp and kill the king, Lars Porsena. So he went. In the Etruscan camp he found that a man was sitting on a high place, dressed in a scarlet robe, and many were coming to him on business. Caius Mucius thought the man was Lars Porsena and drew near him, too. When he was close enough, Caius drew his dagger and stabbed the man, but it was not Lars Porsena; it was his chief officer. Caius Mucius was seized and brought before the King, who asked him who he was.

Said Caius Mucius, "I am a citizen of Rome. Men call me Caius Mucius. As your enemy, I wished to kill you, but I can just as bravely meet death myself. It is the Roman nature to act bravely and to suffer bravely. I am not the only one who has resolved to kill you. Behind me there are many more who all have the same purpose. You will be in this danger every hour of your life from now on."

The King was angry yet afraid. He threatened Caius Mucius that if he didn't tell who these others were and where to find them, he would be burned alive.

"Look!" answered Caius Mucius. "And learn how little we care about our bodies compared with our love for Rome." Then he plunged his right hand into an altar fire and let it burn away without showing any feeling of pain.

The King was astounded. He sprang from his seat and ordered the Roman removed from the altar, then set him free because of his courage. In

The Heroism of Caius Mucius, Bernard Keil (1624–1687), Fundacion Banco Santander, Madrid

return, Caius Mucius told Lars Porsena of 300 noble Roman youths who had vowed, one by one, to seek him out until one succeeded in slaying him. Lars Porsena, then frightened, made peace with Rome and refused to allow the Tarquins to find any further refuge in his kingdom,

After one more fruitless effort to regain the throne, Tarquinius Superbus died in a battle in which the gods, Castor and Pollux, helped Rome to win.

M. CURTIUS

The Samnites were a mountain tribe to the south of Rome. During a war that they fought with Rome for possession of the fertile western plains near the coast, a frightening event took place in Rome. The earth quaked and split, and a great crack widened into a chasm in the middle of the Forum. As the sides of the chasm slipped down, the city as a whole seemed in danger of being swallowed by the earth. The leaders went to the augurs to ask what evil omen this might be and what could be done to regain the favor of the gods. The answer was that if the people wanted to save Rome, they must sacrifice at the chasm that in which lay the strength of Rome.

No one knew what to say. As they were desperately trying to find the meaning of the augurs' words, M. Curtius, a young soldier, spoke up. He asked whether Rome's strength lay elsewhere than in the weapons and courage of Roman men. All became silent. He then looked up to the Capitol and the temples and down into the yawning chasm. Mounting his horse, which was decked for battle, and flourishing his sword, he leapt in full armor into the chasm. Crowds of men and women flung gifts and fruits of the earth in after him. Livy writes that immediately after that the chasm closed.

CAMILLUS AND THE INVASION OF THE GAULS

It was not only the young men who were heroes of Rome. The last war against the Etruscans was a long one. The Romans laid siege to Veii, an Etrurian city not far from Rome. The siege lasted ten years and was not successful until a general named Camillus was made Dictator. Under his leadership, Veii was taken at last.

The Romans then proposed that the lands around Veii be divided amongst the poorer people in Rome. Camillus opposed this, and the citizens then claimed that he hated the poor. He was accused of having taken some of the spoils of battle for himself instead of turning them over to the city.

Camillus, angry, decided to go into exile. He said goodbye to his wife and children and, as he left Rome, he turned. Looking up to the Capitol and praying with outstretched arms to the gods, he vowed that he was not at fault. He pleaded that the people of Rome would call him back when they needed his help again. Every Roman came to believe that what followed was the judgment of the gods against the injustice done to Camillus.

Now, rumors were heard of wild tribes who had appeared on horseback from the mountains of Gaul north of Etruria. The horsemen had swept down into Etruria—fighting, burning and looting as they came closer and closer to Rome. They were tall, fair-haired men with flashing eyes and rough and rude manners. Over their armor they wore heavily embroidered robes, which they threw off when they went into battle; around their necks they wore broad, gold rings as collars.

The Gauls were proud and quarrelsome. Good fighters, they showed no one any mercy. Once they won a fight and had taken all they wanted of an enemy's wealth, they would ride on and attack another city or village. They did not think to take possession of any land. They fought well as long as they won victories, but when defeated, they vanished quickly.

When the Romans heard that the Gauls were only a few miles from Rome, they assembled their entire army and marched forth to meet the barbarians. In a terrific battle, the Romans were defeated and the greater part of their army destroyed. Only a few escaped and fled to Rome to warn the citizens. If the Gauls had immediately marched to Rome, no one there would have escaped with their lives. But the Gauls did not realize that Rome lay just ahead of them. After their battle victory, they feasted and divided up the spoils of battle amongst themselves.

While the Gauls were feasting and resting near Veii, the Romans had time to prepare for them. Some decided to flee, others to stay and meet their fate. But it was also thought that the able-bodied men, the soldiers and senators, should withdraw to the Capitol with the women and children and defend it. Those senators who were too old to fight decided to wait in the city. Many of them had been consuls and generals in their younger days. Dressed in their robes of office, and wearing the insignia of their rank, they seated themselves in ivory chairs in front of their houses to await the enemy.

The Gauls entered an empty, silent city to find only aged Romans sitting in order and in silence along the streets. The Gauls were struck with amazement at the sight of old men who showed no fear. The Gauls were afraid to approach for they thought the Romans must be gods; but one, bolder than the rest, drew near to one elderly senator and, putting forth his hand, stroked the long, white beard. The senator struck the Gaul on the head with a staff, whereupon the Gaul drew his sword and killed the old Roman. The others then followed his example and leaped upon the other senators and killed them all. The invaders sacked and looted the whole city, taking all manner of treasure, and then burned it to the ground.

Now Rome lay in ashes except for the temples on Capitol Hill which were defended still by Roman men. Instead of withdrawing, the Gauls besieged the Capitol for seven months. At last, the Romans called Camillus to their aid, just as he had prayed they would.

Leading a large army of Latins and other men who were anxious to drive the savages out of Italy, Camillus defeated the Gauls in a fierce battle and, as was their custom when defeated, the Gauls fled (390 BC).

"ALL ROADS LEAD TO ROME"

Now Rome was free again, but it was fifty years before she was rebuilt. For another hundred years or so, she was continually at war—with the Samnites, the Latins, and even the Greeks, who were led by a young Greek king, Pyrrhus, who wanted to conquer Italy as Alexander had conquered Persia. Rome was victorious in all her wars and became mistress of all Italy, accomplishing what the Greeks had never been able to do: unite many cities into one nation.

The soldiers of Rome were her citizens who left their farms to fight her wars. The patricians were rewarded with shares in the lands that were conquered. As colonists, they brought the laws and customs of Rome to these new lands. Roads were built from all parts of Italy to Rome, and the conquered people were allowed to trade only with Rome. In this way Rome made sure of her power and influence. Two events are unforgettable parts of this period of Roman history.

To the northeast of Rome, on the slopes of the Appennine Mountains, the Aequian tribe used to come down and plunder Roman lands. One of the Consuls was camped with an army in that region. The Aequians surrounded and besieged the camp as if it were a city. The other Consul had remained in Rome, and he didn't know what to do. The Senate decided to appoint a Dictator.

The Senators chose CINCINNATUS, who had a small farm on the other side of the Tiber. He loved his farm and, although he was a Senator, used to go there whenever he could to dig and plough and to feed and care for his animals. Messengers from the Senate found Cincinnatus at work in his fields. They greeted him and told him to put on his toga, his senatorial garb, so as to receive the message from the Senate. His wife brought him the toga, and after putting it on over the dust and sweat of his farm work, he listened in surprise when the messengers greeted him as Dictator and asked him to come immediately to the city. Thus he went to lead another army and defeated the Aequians. When he returned from the battle, he laid down his dictatorship

Cincinnatus Receiving the Ambassadors from Rome, Alexandre Cabanel (1823–1889), Musée Fabre, 1843

and went back to finish the field work on his farm.

The Plebeians had to fight in Rome's wars. Forced to neglect their farms and businesses and go into debt to make up for their losses, those who couldn't pay their debts were often taken as slaves or put into prison, nor were the lands they helped to conquer shared with them as among the Patricians.

In 494 BC, when a war was expected, the Plebeians all marched out of Rome to a distant hill, Mons Sacer, and announced that they would not fight in the war. The Patricians were alarmed. They needed their soldiers. The Senate sent Menenius Agrippa to plead with them. Agrippa simply told the Plebeians the fable of what happened when the hands, the mouth and the teeth refused to give food to the belly who, to them, seemed to do nothing but enjoy what they provided. When they began to waste away, they could see that the belly was not just living for its own pleasure but that it gave back to the body as strength what it had received as food.

The Secession of the People to the Mons Sacer, B. Barloccini, engraving, 1849

The Plebeians understood the wisdom in this fable and returned to Rome. The Patricians then agreed to cancel the debts of those who served their country and to allow the Plebeians to elect Tribunes to protect them from injustice. It was another hundred years before a law was passed that decreed one of the two Consuls must be a Plebeian.

LATIN PROVERBS

Audi, vidi, tace si vis vivere in pace.
Listen, look, be silent if you would live in peace.

Divide et impera.
Divide and conquer.

Quid licet Jovi, non licit bovi.
What is permitted to Jove is not permitted to the ox.
or, Gods may do what cattle may not.

Justitia est fundamentum regnorum.
Justice is the basis of government.

Ad astra per aspera
Through aspiration to the stars

Errare humanum est.
To err is human.

Honesta fama melior est pecunia.
An honest reputation is better than money.

Imperare sibi maximum imperium est.
To govern oneself is the best form of government.

Finis coronat opus.
The end crowns the work.

Fortes fortuna adiurat.
Fortune helps the strong.

Labor omnia vincit.
Work conquers all.

Nil homini certum est.
Nothing is sure to man.

Non omnia possumus omnes.
Not everyone can do everything.

Pari cum paribus facillime congregandur.
Birds of a feather flock together.

Podior est, qui prior est.
First come, first served.

Quot homines tot sententiae.
As many opinions as people.

Poriculum in mora.
Danger in delay.

Factum fieri in fectum non potest.
You can't undo what is done.

HOW ROME GOVERNED ITALY

Romans believed in the rule of law. Many of their laws have come down to us and we still live under them. We know some of them well:

If you give your word about some business matter, you have to keep it.

If you cannot pay all your debts at once, the payments can be divided fairly among your creditors and be paid off little by little.

All merchants are required to give an honest measure.

Men cannot be punished for a suspected crime. They first have to be proven guilty.

Imperare sibi maximum imperium est. To govern oneself is the best form of government. Such was the belief of the Romans, and that respect for authority at home made Rome fit to rule others.

Via Appia Antica in Rome, photograph, 2005

Rome's methods of governing Italy were such that she became the axle, the center, around which the wheel turned. The conquered tribes spoke different languages and they had different customs. Rome made separate treaties with each tribe so that each was bound directly to Rome and each was made to feel that it was Roman. Great roads were built, like the spokes of the wheel, connecting the separate cities and colonies with Rome. Along these roads from Rome to distant places went those who carried the spirit of Roman law and order. In time, each of the peoples of Italy came to feel: "My native town is but a portion of Rome."

ROME AND CARTHAGE

During the two hundred years when Rome had been busy forming a nation in Italy, the Romans gave little heed to what was happening in the rest of the world. Themistocles, Pericles, Philip of Macedon, Alexander the Great, Aristotle and other Greek leaders lived and died as the power of Rome began to grow. Greek civilization ruled in the eastern Mediterranean, and another great power from the East established itself in the West. Once Rome looked out upon the rest of the world, she found this power right on her doorstep.

What she saw was the commercial empire of the Phoenicians who had fled from Alexander the Great. Their greatest city, Carthage, had been founded by the Phoenician Princess, Dido, who had so loved Aeneas that, when he left Carthage, she had cursed him and had vowed eternal enmity toward him and all his race.

Carthage was a great port for ships of trade. All the trade between Africa, Etruria, Spain and Sicily went through Carthage. Men of all lands traded in Carthage. They had one interest in common—money or gold. The Carthaginians fought to control trade routes by closing their harbor to any ships but their own. Their chief competitors were the Etruscans and the Greeks who had settled in Italy. The Carthaginian army was made up of mercenaries, men of many races and many tongues, who had no special love for Carthage but loved wages, so they were not very trustworthy. Carthaginians believed that there was nothing that money could not buy.

From 264 to 201 BC, Rome and Carthage came into great conflicts with each other which would decide whether the Phoenician (or Punic) power or the Roman power was to become the leading power on earth. These struggles are called the Punic Wars and were led by four personalities who stood out as leaders: one Carthaginian and three Romans.

Hannibal taking the oath, from a jigsaw puzzle, Mary Evans

The Carthaginians had taken possession of Messana, a Greek city in Sicily, and the Greeks called on Rome for help against the invaders. Fearing that they might also try to invade Italy, the Romans fought and defeated the Carthaginians and drove them out of Sicily. The Carthaginian General, HAMILCAR BARKA, became filled with a burning hatred for Rome and vowed to avenge the disgrace he had suffered in defeat. When he tried to raise a new army, the Carthaginians showed no interest and felt no patriotism. So Hamilcar went to Spain hoping to form an army there. Before going he had asked his 9-year-old son, Hannibal, whether he wanted to come with him. Hannibal begged to be allowed to go. Hamilcar took his son to make a sacrifice at the temple, and to have the boy take the vow: "I will never hold friendship with the Romans." Hannibal kept this vow to his dying day.

Hamilcar died in Spain ten years later when HANNIBAL was 19 years old, too young to command an army. But by the time he was 26, he became Commander-in-Chief of the Carthaginian army, and his one aim was to deal death to Rome.

Hannibal won the love of his troops because he was fearless and calm in the face of danger. He never seemed to tire; he slept only when he was not actively busy with his duties and, then, for only a few hours at a time, not caring whether it was day or night, wrapping himself in his cloak and lying on the ground among his soldiers. He dressed in no way differently from his soldiers and was first among them in battle, the first to enter the fight and the last to leave the field.

There had been a truce between Rome and Carthage for 23 years, but now a quarrel arose over a colony of Greeks in Spain. It was protected by

Rome and the only spot in Spain not under the power of Carthage. Hannibal besieged this colony, Saguntum, and won it in eight months. Rome prepared for war.

This was the second Punic War. In 218 BC Rome sent an army by sea, under one of the Consuls, to attack the Carthaginians in Spain. No sooner had the army landed in Spain than it was recalled to Rome because of most unexpected news. Hannibal was invading Italy!

Hannibal had led about 50,000 foot soldiers, 9000 horsemen and 40 elephants by land, north over the Pyrenees, through the south of Gaul and over the Alps into the valley of the Po River. It had taken him fifteen days to cross the Alps, and over half his men died in the severe, cold conditions. Hannibal himself was blinded in one eye, and it is recorded that only one of his elephants survived the trek.

The Carthaginians had fought their way through wild tribes of mountaineers, Gauls and Celts, who sometimes rolled great boulders down on Hannibal's army from the mountain heights and at other times trapped it in narrow passes. Many men and animals slipped over precipices and slid down the cliffs. Horses were frightened by the shouts of attacking Gauls and the baggage animals, heavily laden, rolled over the ledges like falling houses. After nine days Hannibal and his soldiers reached the highest point of the Alps. After climbing the steep, pathless slopes, the troops rested but were filled with fear when it snowed.

Throughout all these misfortunes Hannibal had stayed calm. Now, when he saw that his men were about to give up, he climbed a peak and showed to those who were with him a view of Italy and the rich valley of the Po. He shouted, "You are now crossing, not only into Italy, but into Rome itself. In one or, at the most, two battles, you will be the masters of Rome." The descent into Italy was worse than the climb. It was steeper, more slippery, and many more were lost. Once in the valley, they camped to rest and regain their strength.

The Romans had never dreamed that Hannibal would invade Italy by crossing the Alps. Led by the Consul Scipio, they now hurriedly set out, with a certain amount of dread, to wipe out the Carthaginian camp. Instead, Scipio was wounded, defeated and rescued by his son. The Romans withdrew, were

From *Die Karthager – Hannibals Übergang über die Alpen [The Carthaginians – Hannibal's Crossing the Alps]*, Heinrich Leutemann (1824–1905), Munich, leafsheet of thirteen images from the ancient times, 1866

joined by new forces, attacked again and were defeated again. They returned to Rome.

Hannibal rested in the Po valley for the winter. In Rome men and women were uneasy.

In the spring, Rome sent an army under the Consul Flaminius against Hannibal, but Hannibal had already marched through the spring floods and through Etruria, to position his army between Flaminius and Rome.

He ambushed the Romans and, in a great battle, defeated them utterly and killed Flaminius. At the time of the battle, there was an earthquake that destroyed towns, broke off cliffs and altered river courses; but the fighters did not even notice it, so fiercely were they engaged.

Another great battle at Cannae was lost by the Romans when 70,000 of their 80,000 soldiers were killed. The defeated Consul returned to Rome in despair. If he had been a Carthaginian, he would have been put to torture, but in Rome he was met by thousands of citizens and thanked because he had done his best. The Romans had to send tribute to Carthage, a bushel of golden rings. However, Carthage thought Hannibal was doing so well that she sent him no money and no reinforcements.

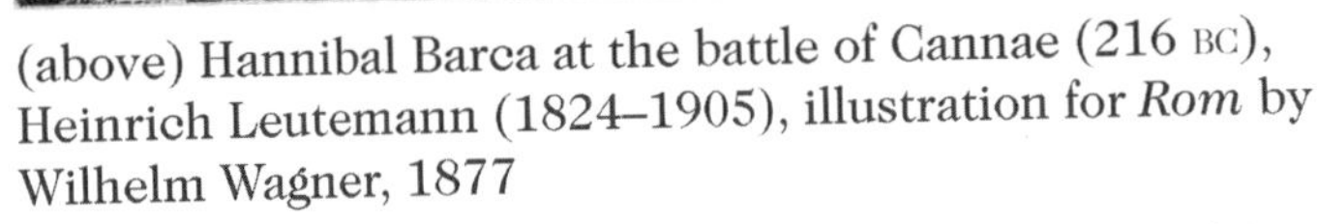

(above) Hannibal Barca at the battle of Cannae (216 BC), Heinrich Leutemann (1824–1905), illustration for *Rom* by Wilhelm Wagner, 1877

(right) Hannibal counting the rings of the Roman knights killed at Cannae, marble, Sébastien Slodtz (French, 1655–1726), Tuileries, Paris, 1704

Two Romans now rose up as leaders: QUINTUS FABIUS MAXIMUS and Publius Scipio. The Senate decided to appoint a Dictator and chose Fabius. He admitted that Hannibal was a greater general than any Roman, but he also knew that Rome had the greater spirit that could not be worn out. He introduced the policy of avoiding battles with Hannibal. He had his army follow Hannibal, harass him, attack him and hide, here a little, there a little. The Romans laid waste to fields so that Hannibal could not supply his troops with grain. Fabius, wanting to weaken Hannibal bit by bit and gradually wear him out, was thought by many Romans to be a coward. They named him Cunctator (the Delayer). For twelve years the Romans struggled, and their spirit never broke. Hannibal, who remained in Italy for these years, never attacked Rome herself but was driven slowly southward. It was a deadlock: Hannibal couldn't conquer Rome and Rome couldn't drive Hannibal out of Italy.

Publius Cornelius Scipio Africanus, Livio Retti (1692–1751), Das Rathaus in Schwäbisch Hall, Württembergisch

Now PUBLIUS SCIPIO, the son of the Scipio who had first met defeat by Hannibal, became Consul. He proposed attacking Carthage. It was agreed. He set sail, reached Africa, made an alliance with an African king, marched against Carthage and defeated her. Carthage sent for Hannibal to come from Italy, although she had never sent him reinforcements or supplies. She now begged for his help. Hannibal was greater than Carthage, so he went and gathered whatever army he could.

Scipio met him in a long, fierce battle at Zama, a few miles south of Carthage and, for the first time in his life, Hannibal was defeated. Peace was

Scipio's triumphal procession to the Jupiter Temple on the Capitol, wool and silk tapestry, Geraert van der Strecke, Royal Castle in Warsaw, 1660

made. Scipio was given a great triumph in Rome and named "Africanus." He was the first commander to be given the name of the people he had conquered.

The terms of the peace were that Rome won Spain and all of the islands between Africa and Italy. Carthage had to give up all her ships of war and all her elephants and pay Rome a yearly tribute of 200 talents (coins); 500 Carthaginian trading ships were towed by the Romans into the harbor and burned. Carthage was left free as a nation to rule herself, yet forbidden to go to war without the permission of Rome.

The third Punic War took place, about fifty years later, in 143 BC, when Rome found out that Carthage was breaking the treaty and rearming to fight a Numidian prince who was a friend of Rome. Rome sent another army to Africa and besieged Carthage for two years and finally burned the city to the ground. The ground where Carthage had stood was salted and ploughed under and a solemn curse laid upon anyone who would ever attempt to rebuild her. Thus, Rome became mistress of the Western Mediterranean.

And what happened to Hannibal? He left Carthage and spent the rest of his life in exile in the East. There, Scipio Africanus met him in later years at the court of an Eastern king. They talked together, these two, and Scipio asked Hannibal, "Whom do you consider the greatest Commander in the world?"

Hannibal answered, "Alexander."

"Who the second greatest?" asked Scipio.

"Pyrrhus."

"Who the third?"

And Hannibal answered, "Myself."

Scipio smiled and asked, "What would you say if you had vanquished me?"

"In that case," said Hannibal, "I would say that I was greater than Alexander, Pyrrhus and all the Commanders in the world."

MARCUS PORCIUS CATO 234–149 BC

Marcus Porcius Cato was a Patrician, a Senator, at one time a Consul, and at one time a Censor.

Who were the Censors? They were Patrician officers elected to number the people, take account of their property, judge their behavior and reduce their rank if they were found guilty of cruelty to their families, extravagance, or dishonesty, or deemed in any way unworthy. The Censors could also increase a man's taxes by setting any value they chose upon his vineyards, olive orchards, carriages, jewels and slaves. A Censor had almost as much power as a dictator.

For 52 years after Hannibal was defeated, Carthage had grown more and more prosperous, and the Romans had grown more and more anxious and jealous. Then when they heard that Carthage was preparing to fight against the King of Numidia without Rome's consent, the Romans sent a commission to Carthage to enquire into the matter. Marcus Cato was a member of this commission. When he returned from Carthage, he said to the Senate, "Carthage, methinks, ought to be utterly destroyed." He said this so often that the Senate agreed and finally, three years after Cato had died, sent the army that destroyed Carthage in the Third Punic War.

During Cato's lifetime, Rome had become increasingly interested in pleasure and luxury. This was not pleasing to him. He had been brought up as a farmer. At the age of 17, he had fought in the army against Hannibal and under the great Roman Generals in other campaigns in Africa, Spain and the East. He had despised the luxury-loving people of the East and Carthage. He had urged the destruction of Carthage, and now the very thing he despised, the search for pleasure rather than duty to the State, was happening in Rome.

In the Eastern Mediterranean, three parts of Alexander's Empire had become three separate kingdoms: Macedonia, Syria and Egypt. Rome found out that the Kings of Macedonia and Syria were plotting to seize Egypt and divide it between them.

As Egypt supplied Rome with grain, the Romans sent an army against the Macedonians and, in Thessaly in 197 BC, defeated the Macedonian King Philip and set the Greek cities free from his rule. The Syrian King Antiochus entered Greece to attack the Roman garrisons that had been left to guard Greek liberty. The Romans drove the Syrians out of Greece into Asia Minor where, at Magnesia in 190 BC, they defeated Antiochus. These things happened during Cato's lifetime. After his death, Syria became the Roman province of Asia.

In the meantime, the Greek cities were again threatened by Perseus, the son of Philip, who sought to win them back from Roman influence. The Consul, Aemilius Paulus, defeated Perseus in 168 BC, and Greece and Macedonia also became Roman provinces.

The Romans took possession of Greece, but the culture of Greece took possession of Rome. Romans began to adopt Greek methods of education, especially the study of philosophy, poetry and the art of speaking in public. The teachers were Greek slaves.

Cato refused to have a Greek slave teach his son. Rather, he taught the boy himself: grammar, law, and gymnastic exercises. He taught him to throw darts, to ride, to fight in armor, to box, to endure heat and cold, to swim through the most rapid and rough rivers. Cato wrote out histories in large letters, so his son could learn about his countrymen and forefathers without leaving the house. Cato wanted the Greek teachers to go home and leave the Romans alone so Roman children would remain obedient to their own laws and governors and not ask too many questions.

Cato made use of slaves on his farm. They had hard and heavy work. Their food and clothing were limited. They were allowed sour wine in small quantities, only those olives that dropped of themselves to the ground, one tunic and one cloak every two years, and a new pair of shoes once in two years. Cato believed that worn out cattle, sick sheep, broken tools, old and sick slaves, and all other useless things should be sold.

During the wars with Hannibal, Rome had always been in danger of defeat. Every bit of what little treasures the people owned was needed to pay for food and armor for the soldiers. A law was passed that forbade any woman to have in her possession more than half an ounce of gold or to wear

Ancient Roman portrait, *Cato and Portia*, Carlo Brogi (1850–1925), Vatican Museum, early 20th century

a dress of several colors, or to ride in a two-horse chariot unless she were going to take part in some religious worship. This was called the Oppian Law.

When the wars were over and Rome began to enjoy prosperity through her trade with the East, many people thought the Oppian Law should be repealed, but others thought it was a good law and that it would help the Romans to remain a self-sacrificing people. For a time, those who argued for and against the law crowded into the Forum to have their say.

The women crowded in too, although the magistrates and the women's husbands forbade it. The women filled all the streets and blocked all the entrances to the Forum. As the men tried to pass them, the women shouted at them to change the law, "for wasn't Rome richer now by reason of her conquests?" The women even sought out the praetors (judges) with their demands that the law be changed. Women from the country towns swarmed into Rome to join the city women.

Marcus Cato was one of the Consuls at the time, and the women with their demands annoyed him. He thought they were interfering too much in men's business. "If you allow women an equal voice in affairs with men," he said, "they will soon become men's masters."

The women, however, were helped by a Tribune who spoke for them, and Cato's advice was, this time, unheeded. The law was repealed, and the women got back their right to fine clothes, golden jewels and two-horse chariots.

THE ROMAN CIRCUS

The Latin word *circus* means "circle" or "ring." In ancient Rome, a circus was for games and contests, and the word *circus* has come to mean what happens in the circle, the show itself. Roman life now had taken on the aspects of a show, a spectacle that can be viewed with awe. What took place in the circus places—the games, the contests and even the races—were of a nature to repel the self-disciplined Greeks. Even those under Roman dominion never accepted the circus, but dismissed it as excessive.

Romans who had become governors of conquered provinces tried to get as much money as they could out of the people of each conquered territory and returned to Rome to make a great display of their wealth. All those who were rich lived in luxury and provided entertainment for the poor who looked to the rich for their support and who would vote for the one who could best feed and clothe them.

When the Romans captured Tarentum, a Greek colony in the south of Italy, they took as a slave an educated Greek named Livius Andronicus who quickly learned Latin and translated some Greek plays into Latin. The Romans gave him a theater on the Aventine Hill and went in crowds

Roman chariot race, from an illustrated school history, illustrator unknown, 1876

Gladiator schooling, mosaic

to see his plays. Then they took an interest in watching animals: Lions, leopards, panthers, and elephants, which they captured in Africa and shipped to Rome, were turned loose in the arenas and people could watch them fight and kill each other. This was popular entertainment, but only for awhile. It gradually became boring. It was more exciting to see men fight and kill each other.

These men were called gladiators, a name taken from the Latin word *gladius*, meaning "sword." Gladiators were usually slaves or criminals, who were promised their freedom if they would fight in the arenas for a certain number of years without being slain. These men were really fighting for their lives, for their freedom. They fought each other clumsily, in desperation, and this began to bore the spectators. Schools for fighting gracefully were set up, where the gladiators had to train and from which they could be called upon to fight in the arena. If a gladiator won a combat, he would stand proudly beside his victim. If he had shown bravery and grace of movement in the fight, the spectators would hold up their thumbs and he would leave the arena alive. However, if the spectators felt that he had fought awkwardly, or had shown fear, their thumbs were pointed downward. Then the winner would be put to death where he stood.

THE GRACCHI

What had become of the blessings that Numa Pompilius had tried to bestow on the Romans—the blessing of friendly, human exchange, love of the gods, the peaceful occupation of working on one's own land with one's own hands? Instead, certain powerful people, even some senators, were greedy, and they took land from the peasants who were away fighting for Rome. When the peasant-soldiers returned, their farms had been taken over, and they were not even allowed to work on what was once their own land. Many of these men and their families became homeless and didn't have enough to eat.

This situation troubled certain people and among these were two brothers who were born to a wise mother, Cornelia, the daughter of Scipio

Cornelia, madre dei Gracchi [Cornelia, Mother of the Gracchi Brothers], Joseph-Benoît Suvée (1743–1807), Louvre Museum, 1795.

Africanus. Cornelia made certain that her sons, Tiberius and Gaius, were educated. She brought excellent tutors from Greece to teach her sons. The boys learned about democracy and the ideals of the Roman Republic. They were fine students.

Once a friend visited Cornelia to show her some beautiful jewels that she had acquired. When the friend asked Cornelia if she would show her the jewels she owned, Cornelia said, "Wait awhile." When Tiberius and Gaius came home from school, she showed them to the lady, saying, "These are my jewels."

When these "jewels" were grown up, they wanted to bring Rome to its senses. They cared about all the people in Rome, so they decided to do something about the situation. Tiberius became a tribune and began to restore land to the peasants. He also made grain cheaper to purchase and even paid for clothes for the poorest of them. Many of the senators were not happy about this. These men gathered a mob together, marched into the Forum, and had Tiberius and 300 of his men beaten until they died. This was the first time there had been bloodshed of this kind in over 400 years.

Ten years later, Gaius became a tribune. He courageously continued the land reform. For two years he was successful, until a mob was raised to kill him too. Later over 3000 of his followers were arrested and sentenced to die. From then on, most of the leaders of Rome controlled the Empire as much by force and fear as by good leadership.

MARIUS AND SULLA

One unfortunate result of the Gracchi's land reform and grain laws was that many people stopped wanting to work and were ready to follow anyone, vote for anyone, who would promise to give them what they wanted. The Senate took more and more power as an assembly of the people became impossible because citizens were now too numerous and scattered. Under these conditions could Rome govern herself successfully, let alone the distant lands under her dominion?

Over and over again she had to send out armies to subdue revolts in Africa, in Greece, in Asia. The generals of one such army came home without fighting because the enemy had bribed them with gold. The Roman Senate took little notice of this, but the people were indignant and elected Caius Marius as Consul. Marius was a young officer who had served under Scipio Africanus. He promised to capture an African leader of such a revolt, and he did. He became so popular then, that, without regard for the law limiting Consuls to one year in office, he was re-elected the following year, and again for a third and a fourth year, seven times in all.

Caius Marius Amid the Ruins of Carthage, John Vandelyn (1775–1852), painting, Fine Arts Museum of San Francisco, 1807

As Consul, Marius became Commander-in-Chief of the army, and for the first time, Rome was ruled by military power, not by popular vote. The army too had changed because Rome waged war far from her own shores and because there were fewer farmers and free men working on their own land; city men didn't feel like fighting for Rome with no land to defend. So Marius trained a paid army. The soldiers were known as "Marius' mules." They had to carry their own baggage and prepare their own food, and they were hired from all over the Roman world. It was as if Carthage had won, as if her spirit had triumphed over the Roman spirit now that her gold had made Rome rich.

With his army, Marius saved Rome from danger of new invasions from the north and defeated two barbarian tribes who were advancing into Italy. It was a great victory that he won when he destroyed the Teutones and the Cimbri. His fifth consulship was his reward, and he entered Rome in triumph. From being a brave and simple soldier he now changed, seeking more and more power for himself instead of thinking of the good of Rome.

After his victories Marius had to act as Consul, not as Commander-in-Chief. In the year of his sixth consulship, the Romans were more and more at swords' points with each other, the Senators on one side and the people on the other. There were rioting and bloodshed in the streets. Marius could not stop it. He wasn't as wise as Numa Pompilius. The people longed for a real leader who would put an end to injustice. They blamed Marius, whom they had but recently worshipped as a god. At the end of his sixth consulship, Marius left Rome and went to Asia.

During this time, a Roman citizen, wherever he went, was protected by the laws of Rome. The Italians wanted citizenship, but the Romans still denied it to them. In 91 BC, Marcus Drucus tried to make a law granting it, but he was murdered, just as the Gracchi had been. The Italians then set up a rival power to Rome, and a war started which lasted for two years.

Marius came back and fought for Rome, but now he was outshone by a new, young officer, Lucius Cornelius Sulla, who won more victories. Marius became jealous, and he and Sulla soon grew to hate each other. Sulla was elected Consul by the nobles.

Rome won the war against the Italians, not only by force of arms but also by granting them citizenship on the condition that they would lay down their weapons within sixty days. The Romans realized that they needed the loyalty of the Italians.

Still ambitious for himself, Marius now found another enemy in addition to Sulla, who wanted to be the chief power. An eastern king, Mithridates, had appeared in Asia and was moving westward, threatening the Roman provinces. In 88 BC Marius and Sulla, the two leading generals, each wanted to lead the Roman army to fight with Mithridates. The Senate, now made up of rich men, appointed Sulla. The Assembly of the people in Rome chose Marius. Which was to lead?

Sulla, who was already at the head of a large army he had built while Marius was in Asia, marched into Rome and settled the question by force. Never before had such a thing happened in Rome. Now it was clear: Rome was not ruled by either the Senate or the Assembly, but by the man who could command an army.

Sulla went east. Marius was banished from Rome, but no ships would take him, so he went into hiding in Italy. No Roman could bring himself to kill Caius Marius, so a Gallic slave was hired. He found Marius in a dark hut in a little Italian town. When the slave approached, he was frightened, for Marius' eyes seemed to dart flames at him, and he heard a loud voice, "Fellow, darest thou kill Caius Marius?" The Gaul rushed out of the hut in fear. So Marius escaped. He went to Carthage, or where it once stood, but the Roman governors in Africa would not give him refuge.

New fights started in Rome between the nobles and the people. Marius returned and took the part of the people. He gave himself over to revenge and led his troops not only against armed men, but also against unarmed men, murdering them in cold blood, killing all whom he thought had been or were opposed to him. Then Marius, now 70 years old, named himself Consul. It was his seventh consulship.

When Sulla returned, victorious over Mithridates, Marius knew that this meant another struggle and possible banishment. He became anxious, couldn't sleep at night, and, at the news that Sulla was drawing near, he became ill and died on the 17th day of his 7th consulship, in the year 86 BC.

Sulla had been absent from Rome for three years, during which time he had driven Mithridates (who called himself King of Kings) back to his own kingdom. Sulla had punished all those cities, including Athens, who had received the Easterner and allowed him power. In these three years Sulla and his army had killed 160,000 human beings.

An historian has described Sulla as having eyes of a pure and piercing blue, but their expression was sinister and frightening, especially as his complexion was coarse; his face was marked with pimples and blotches. The Greeks compared it to a mulberry sprinkled with meal. His manners were haughty and morose. He seemed always angry. In any history of him there is no mention of a single act of kindness or generosity. The Roman nobles, who accepted him as their champion and who supported his power, had no personal liking for him. He in turn had nothing but contempt for mankind; he did not feel that men were worth respect. Yet he loved pleasures, feasting, and drinking, and he surrounded himself with dancers and jesters and buffoons who knew how to make fun of other men.

In 83 BC, Sulla sailed from Macedonia across to the east coast of Italy and started his march to Rome. On July 6, while Sulla was marching thus, there was a sudden catastrophe in Rome. The Capitol was destroyed by a fire, the holy places of Rome and the Sibylline Books devoured by flames. No one ever found out what caused the fire. This destruction of the Temples and Oracles seemed to be the sign of a great change in the destiny of Rome, and it actually marked the end of the Republic.

Sulla came back to Rome expecting a triumph, but the new consul, a commoner, who was in Marius' place, opposed his return and sent an army to keep him out of Italy. Sulla fought his way through to Rome and entered the city as its master. His first act was to issue an order that all who had opposed his return should be killed. Then began the bloodiest page of Roman history. It is called "The Reign of Terror."

Not only those who might have opposed Sulla were killed, but many thousands more. At Sulla's command, his soldiers killed people on the streets, in their houses, in the Forum and in the countryside. Men were killed as they left their homes for work, women were killed as they tended their children, even babes were killed in their mothers' arms. No one knew who was safe or in danger.

A question was asked of Sulla in the Senate: "Whom shall we keep to enjoy our victory if the blood flows in our cities as abundantly as on the battlefield?" Another request was, "Spare not the guilty but reassure those you plan to spare." Sulla coldly replied that he had not yet decided whom he would spare.

"Then warn us of those who are to be punished," the Senate asked.

Thereafter lists of those who were to be killed were posted for all to read. Each day Sulla would remember the names of more people to add to the "proscription." Some of Sulla's favorites made money by taking him the names of people whom others wanted murdered. These were added to the lists. Then Sulla turned against those very rich men who had first made him Consul and killed them so he could enrich himself with their farmlands and palaces.

Sulla views the list of proscribed, engraving from a drawing by Silvestre David Mirys (1742–1810), France, 1799

From December 1 to June 1, 82 BC, the slaughter of Romans continued, not only in Rome, but also throughout the large cities of Italy. Many native tribes perished. Their languages and customs disappeared with them. For example, the civilization of Etruria disappeared—to be forgotten for two thousand years, then rediscovered in our time in the buried graves of that land.

The relatives of Caius Marius were hunted down after the body of Marius had been torn from its grave and thrown into the river. This crime shocked and offended the people who said that Marius' ghost was haunting the spot to frighten countrymen whenever a calamity occurred. One relative of Marius, named Marius Gratidianus, was beheaded by one of Sulla's officers and his head placed on Sulla's banquet table.

An 18-year-old nephew of the wife of Marius was married to Cornelia, the daughter of Cinna, one of Sulla's enemies. When Sulla demanded that the young man divorce his wife, he refused and fled to the Sabine Mountains. Sulla sent men after him to kill him, but this young man's time to die had not yet come. Kinsmen of his and the Vestal women went to Sulla to plead for his life. Even some of Sulla's own followers spoke in his favor.

Sulla gave in, saying, "I spare him but beware! In that young trifler there is more than one Marius." So this young man escaped with his life. His name was Julius Caesar.

At last the reign of terror ended. Sulla forced the people to make him Dictator; then he set about changing the form of government to destroy what remained of the Republic. He ruled by decree. Consuls could still be elected but had to obey the Dictator. Tribunes, if elected, could never take any higher office after that; they could not vote or suggest laws in the Senate. In the proscriptions, 200 senators had been killed and replaced by 300 soldiers who had fought with Sulla. Any new senators were to be the sons of these men, a hereditary succession. Sulla gave Roman citizenship to 10,000 slaves so as to increase the number of his followers.

In 79 BC, Sulla was now old. Believing that none had been favored by the gods as much as he, he called himself "Sulla the Fortunate" and retired to a villa at Cumae. To celebrate his retirement, he used a tenth of his wealth to pay for a great feast for the people. So much food was left over that vast heaps of it were shoveled into the river. He returned to a life of pleasure surrounded by entertainers. He feasted, drank, read the literature of Greece and dictated the memoirs of his life, in which he said that it had been prophesied in his youth that he would die after a happy life at the very height of his prosperity.

In a dream, he said, his dead son appeared to him and begged him to rest from his troubles and come to join him to dwell in eternal peace and tranquility. Then Sulla died in 78 BC at the age of 60. He was given a magnificent funeral in the Campus Martius and buried there in the Field of Mars, the God of War. The inscription on his tomb reads: "None of his friends ever did him a kindness, and none of his foes a wrong, without being generously repaid."

THE FIRST TRIUMVIRATE

After Sulla's death, three men rose to leadership in Rome: Pompey, Crassus and Julius Caesar. They made an agreement between them to share in governing Rome and her provinces. So it came about that, instead of two consuls, three triumvirs exercised authority in the affairs of the Romans.

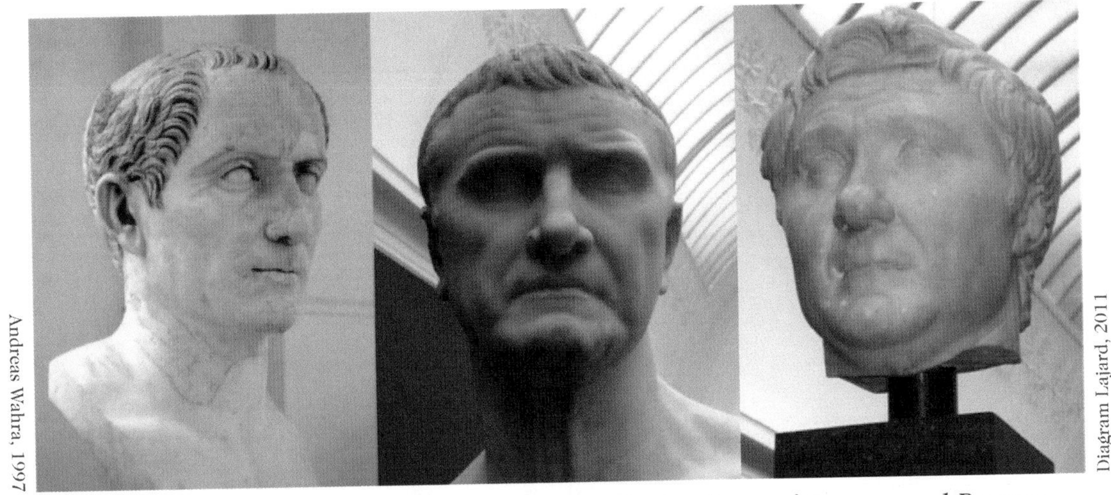
Andreas Wahra, 1997

Diagram Lajard, 2011

Bust of *Caesar,* National Archaeological Museum, Naples; Busts of *Crassus* and *Pompey*, Ny Carlsberg Glyptothek, Copenhagen

POMPEY had won fame as a general through his victories over the followers of Marius in Africa and Sicily. While Rome was busy with civil wars, pirates had gained control of the seas and were looting merchant ships. The pirate ships had golden masts, purple sails and silver-plated oars. Pompey was assigned to clear the seas of the pirates, which he did in forty days with 500 ships at his command; 400 pirate ships were captured, thirteen destroyed and not a Roman ship was lost.

Mithridates had become strong again, and Pompey was sent against him with full authority as would a king. He conquered Mithridates and established the Roman world from the Euphrates and the Red Sea to the Atlantic Ocean. He was called upon to put down the danger of a revolt in Spain and was made Governor of Spain.

CRASSUS was the richest man in Rome, but it was said that he'd gotten rich on other's misfortunes. When Spartacus, a Thracian leader who had been sold as a slave, led a revolt of the gladiators, it was Licinius Crassus who led the Romans in overcoming the rebels, killing and crucifying Spartacus and 6000 of his followers. As one of the triumvirs, Crassus was then sent to Asia Minor to govern Rome's eastern provinces.

JULIUS CAESAR was a follower of Marius. All of his sympathies were with the people, and he spoke out for them often enough to win their favor and to lose the favor of the Senate. Perhaps to get rid of him, he was sent as Pro-Consul to Gaul. During a period of nine years he conquered all of Gaul.

When Crassus was slain in the East, Pompey (with his army) was in Rome and Caesar with his army was in Gaul. Although Pompey's wife, Julia, was Caesar's daughter, Pompey felt enmity toward Caesar. When Julia died, Pompey began to raise up enemies against Caesar in Rome. In the struggle between the Senate and the people, Pompey was on the side of the Senate.

JULIUS CAESAR 100-44 BC

Julius Caesar was born of a noble family, a descendant of Aeneas, hence of the Goddess Venus. He is described as having been tall and fair with black, lively eyes. He was neat in dress, his face was shaven, and he was partially bald-headed but combed his back hair forward over the bald spot. He loved jewels and fine food. He liked to spend money lavishly, and when he had spent all his own, he borrowed from friends. He sold Roman titles to foreign princes for gold to pay for extravagant shows in the circus and for slaves (as long as they were handsome).

Julius Caesar, Nicholas Coustou (1658–1733), commissioned in 1696 for the Gardens at Versailles, Louvre Museum

Caesar was a great orator; he had studied with a Greek teacher. He was also a great general. He wrote his own account of his campaigns in Gaul and elsewhere, which gives us much of Roman history. He was a perfect master of all weapons and a complete horseman. He never gave in to fatigue and always marched at the head of his troops, most often on foot. His head was bare in all kinds of weather. Often in disguise, he would travel into enemy lines alone to see what his battle plan should be. He never let an enemy have time to regain strength, but always drove it out of its camp after a victory. If a victory seemed doubtful, Caesar would have the horses of all his officers taken away so they wouldn't have the means to make a quick escape.

He rode a special horse, which he himself had bred, with feet almost like those of a man for its hooves were divided as if into toes. Fortune tellers had said that whoever possessed this horse would become master of the world. The horse would not carry anyone but Caesar. Yet Caesar paid little heed to prophecies and omens, good or bad, and would say, "I will choose my own omens."

He never valued a soldier because he was rich or of noble birth but only according to his strength. He addressed his men not as "soldiers" but as "fellow soldiers." He loved his troops so much that, when one of his armies suffered a certain defeat, he neither cut his hair nor shaved his beard until he had avenged the defeat. Hence, his soldiers loved him. This made them so brave that, even with their smaller numbers, they were able to overcome armies of greater numbers. One brave soldier of Caesar's maintained his post as guard of a gate in a fort to the end of the battle, and when it was over, he had lost an eye and had been run through the thigh and through the shoulder; his shield had been pierced in 120 places.

Caesar always treated his friends with good nature and kindness. Once when one of them became ill on a journey through a forest, Caesar gave him the only sheltered spot to sleep in that night, and Caesar himself slept outdoors on the ground. In any quarrel with another, Caesar was always ready to forgive or to make up the difference betwixt them. One man who had written some insulting words against Caesar, then begged his pardon, and Caesar immediately invited the man to have supper with him that same night. On the other hand, Caesar did not hesitate to watch the blood flow in the great sports shows when gladiators fought to the death as people applauded.

Since Sulla's death, Julius Caesar, as leader of the popular party, had for eighteen years hoped and tried to bring Rome back to greatness and honor without the help of an army. As Pro-Consul in Gaul, with many troops under him, he had suggested that he would disband his army and come back to Rome to win a consulship by means of an election if Pompey would agree to do likewise. Pompey refused. Caesar then saw that he could not achieve anything for Rome except at the head of an army that would fight for him; he was already 40 years old.

When the Senate sent orders for Caesar to disband his army or be declared an enemy of Rome, he called his army together and asked the men to support him against the Senate. The soldiers called for action, and Caesar led them toward Italy.

The River Rubicon marked the border between Caesar's part of Gaul and Italy. The law was that the Rubicon could not be crossed by anyone in command of an army. Now, as he stood by the banks of the Rubicon, Caesar was thoughtful and said to those who stood near him, "Even yet we may turn back; but once we cross yon little bridge, the whole question will have to be decided by the sword."

As he hesitated in doubt, there appeared nearby a being of marvelous size and beauty who sat on a rock playing a shepherd's pipe. The soldiers gathered around it to listen, among them some trumpeters. The being snatched a trumpet from one of them and blew a mighty blast on the trumpet—the call to war—and strode across the river to the other side.

Then Caesar cried out, "Take we the course which the signs of the gods point out. The die is cast!" *Alia iacta est!* Then he led his legions across the river to begin the swift march to Rome. He took cities without bloodshed, as the people, remembering Sulla, fled in fear.

Pompey, who had been made sole consul by the Senate, left Rome before Caesar got there. He fled to the East with the thought that there he could enlist more troops, free himself from Rome and win power over the larger part of Roman possessions. Caesar entered and took command of Rome. The people's great question was: "How will he treat his enemies?"

When Caesar was told that one of his old friends had gone with Pompey, he only ordered that his money and belongings be sent after him. Caesar took the government into his own hands and was made Dictator. He called back people who had fled from Sulla, made certain new laws that did away with injustices and, as one day followed another, the Romans began to breathe freely again, for no man lost his life or suffered any cruelty.

Pompey gained control of the Eastern lands from which grain could be shipped for the Italians. Caesar knew he could not obtain food for Italy so long as Pompey was in power in the East.

The next battlefield for the Romans was spread out over the whole Mediterranean world, with Pompey on one side ready to fight for personal power and Caesar on the other. For what did Caesar strive? Was it to establish the Roman spirit? Was it love for Rome, for law, for selflessness in duty? Greece, Egypt, Africa and Spain were to be Caesar's battlefields.

Pursuing Pompey into Greece, Caesar fought him twice and defeated him. Though Pompey won a victory in the first battle, he did not conclude it and allowed Caesar to escape him. In the next encounter Pompey lost the fight and fled to Egypt. Pompey was defeated mainly because his soldiers were Easterners, and his officers, though devoted to him, were neither loyal to Rome nor to each other. During the second battle, it is said, Caesar pointed out a young soldier in Pompey's line and gave orders to his own men to be careful of the young man's life. When the victory was won, this young man was, among others, pardoned and treated well. He was given an office in the Roman government and treated as if he were Caesar's own son. His name was Marcus Brutus.

After Pompey fled Greece, Caesar entered Pompey's camp and found banquet tables set for a victory celebration. He also found all the letters from men who had pretended to be his friends, which they had written to Pompey, informing him of Caesar's plans. Even though Caesar knew the names of the writers were in the letters, he threw the whole bundle, unread, into the fire.

Pompey went to Alexandria, then ruled by a Ptolemy, a descendant of Alexander's cousin Ptolemy. This ruler was but a boy. His advisors were afraid that Caesar would be angry if Egypt gave Pompey refuge and that Pompey would be angry if they didn't give him refuge. When Caesar arrived in Egypt, the Egyptian leaders brought him a present—Pompey's head. Caesar was horrified, turned away from it and wept. He wrote a letter to friends in Rome about this sad event, saying, "My greatest and only pleasure in victory is to save the lives of those who have fought against me."

Having placed Cleopatra, the princess, on the throne instead of her young brother, Caesar left Egypt and went to Asia Minor to fight the son of Mithridates. He reported his victory there in three words, "*Veni, vidi, vici.*"*

*"I came, I saw, I conquered."

Caesar Giving the Cleopatra the Throne of Egypt, Pietro de Cortona (1596–1669), Museum of Fine Arts of Lyon, 1637

Next he went back to North Africa against some of Pompey's followers and subdued them, and then to Spain against Pompey's sons. Now the whole Roman world was freed from the dangers of disturbance and revolt. Caesar returned to Rome in 45 BC, was received in great triumph, and made Dictator for life. Little did anyone foresee that his lifetime was to be very short.

How did he govern? He pardoned his enemies, made no favorites of his friends, and increased the number of senators. He made new laws regarding the distribution of grain and new laws for the just settlement of debts. He encouraged the founding of colonies and gave Roman citizenship to people from some of the conquered provinces outside of Italy. He reformed the calendar by allotting a certain number of days to each month just as we number them in our present period of history.

What did he plan? He planned and hoped to improve the harbor of Ostia, to erect beautiful buildings in Rome, to collect a great library of Greek and Roman books, to gather all Roman laws into one book of law, to build roads and canals in the provinces and to drain marshy lands and make them arable. He was determined to use the great wealth that had come to Rome through his conquests for the greatness of Rome.

Julius Caesar was honored as no one had been honored before him. The nobles offered him the title of *Imperator*, or Emperor. He refused it, saying, "My name is Caesar, not Emperor." People respected him for that. His person was declared sacred and from that time on, he gave up his bodyguard and went about accompanied only by unarmed friends. He was called "the Father of his Country," was given a throne of ivory and gold, and statues of him were placed in temples as if he were a god. The month of Quintilus was renamed July in his honor. Throughout the year his victory days were celebrated as holidays, with games and sacrifices, and every five years, a special day of prayer was to be set aside when the priests and the Vestals were to offer up public prayers for his safety.

Most men would have lost their heads in such a situation, accepted the crown as Emperor, become tyrannical, willful and self-seeking. Caesar remained undisturbed, kind and gracious to all. Before a year was up, the Roman people were more devoted to him than they had been to any of their previous rulers.

A few men, however, did not trust him. They believed he would use his power selfishly in the end. Perhaps they envied him. For one reason or another they were against him but kept it secret. Their leaders were two men whom Caesar had pardoned after the defeat of Pompey. One was named Cassius, the other Brutus, Marcus Brutus. These were the men who suggested Caesar be give the title of Emperor in the hopes that this would make the people turn against him.

February 15th was the day that the Lupercalia was always celebrated in honor of Lupercal, a nature god and patron of agriculture. At the rites and festivities, Julius Caesar was seated on the gold and ivory throne. A man approached him and drew forth, from his robe, a crown which he offered to Caesar as a gift from the Roman people. The eyes of the multitude were upon him, a few faint hand-claps were heard, then a displeased silence. Caesar raised his hand and pushed the crown away. Again the man offered it, again Caesar refused and spoke, "I am not the emperor. The only emperor of the Romans is Jupiter." Then he ordered that the crown be taken to Jupiter's temple on Capitol Hill and placed there where it belonged.

The men who were conspiring against Caesar found others to join their ranks: seventy to eighty men, many of whom had accepted high office from Caesar and had been honored and favored by him. Marcus Brutus, the chief of these conspirators, claimed to be a descendant of the Brutus who had been one of the first two consuls of Rome. Marcus Brutus had accepted every honor that Caesar had given him, and he enjoyed the sense of glory that he felt in Caesar's presence. His love of power was flattered when the conspirators named him as their chief advisor.

On the 14th of March, Caesar was dining with friends and the talk was of death. One asked, "What is the best way to die?" Caesar answered, "The best death is that which is sudden and unexpected. It is better to die once than to be always in fear of death."

That night Caesar's wife had bad dreams which so frightened her that the next day, March 15th, she begged Caesar not to leave home to go to the Senate. This fifteenth of March, the Ides, or middle of the month, was the day an augur had warned him against. One day, in the street, this augur had pressed through the crowd toward Caesar and cried out, "Beware the Ides of March!" His wife reminded Caesar of this, but it was not Caesar's way to abide omens, and he set forth unafraid.

Along his way, many people crowded around him, as was usual, pressing upon him written petitions or accounts of their troubles. One such man, a Greek and a friend of Caesar, put a note in his hand begging him to read it without delay, This note told of certain suspicions held by the Greek who, the night before, had been a guest in the house of one of the conspirators. Caesar was prevented from reading it by the pressing crowd, but he kept it in his hand.

As Caesar entered the Senate Building, all senators rose to receive him. His chair had been placed below the pedestal of a statue of Pompey, and Caesar was led to it by those men who most plotted against him. As soon as he was seated, one man came forward and started to plead for his brother

The Death of Julius Caesar, Vincenzo Camuccini (1771–1844), Galleria Nazionale d'Arte Moderna, oil on canvas, 1804

who was in exile, that he might be recalled and pardoned. Caesar answered that this request could not be considered as yet.

Then the man seized hold of Caesar's purple robe and cried out, "Friends, what are you waiting for?" This was a signal which was answered at once. More than a dozen men rushed upon Caesar with daggers drawn. He tried to defend himself but he was surrounded. Whichever way he turned, he was stabbed. As he caught the hand of the first man, who had stabbed him in the breast, another struck a dagger into his side. Cassius stabbed him in the face, and a fourth man drove a dagger right through his thigh. As this happened, Caesar saw that it was the dagger wielded by Brutus, whom he had befriended. To him Caesar now turned, saying, "Et tu, Brute!" and then stopped defending himself. He drew his robe up over his face and fell, helpless and bleeding. Nor did the murderers stop then, but continued to stab him until there were 23 wounds in his body and his life was gone. His blood bathed the pedestal of Pompey's statue.

When the awful deed was done, the senators fled from the building and left Caesar where he had fallen. Crowds gathered and, when they heard the news that Caesar was dead, there was great confusion. Brutus claimed, before the people, that another Tarquinius had been vanquished by another Brutus, but so great was the fury of the people that they were not impressed by Brutus's apology. They rushed through the city and set fire to the houses of the murderers, who fled out of Rome.

Then the people erected a great funeral pyre in the Forum, in front of the palace of the ancient kings of Rome. Placing Caesar's body on it, they set it afire, and the people remained by it throughout the night. Mark Antony, one of Caesar's friends, read Caesar's will. He left his gardens to the city of Rome for the use of the people, a sum of money was left to every citizen, and he named as his heir Caius Julius Caesar Octavianus, better known as Octavian.

Soon Caesar was ranked as a god for, at the first games celebrated in his memory, a comet appeared in the heavens and was seen there every night for seven nights. It was believed to be the soul of Julius Caesar.

> You brought the nations one great Fatherland,
> You raised the savage with your taming hand,
> Broke him, but gave him laws to be his aid.
> A city of the scattered earth you made.
>
> – Rutilius Claudius Namatianus,
> early 5th century AD poet

CAESAR AUGUSTUS 63 BC–14 AD

In Illyria, across the Adriatic Sea, an 18-year-old boy was studying with a Greek teacher. He was a special sort of boy because he was the grand-nephew and adopted son of Julius Caesar. He was called Octavian.*

One day he received a letter from his mother begging him to flee far to the east without delay in order to escape all danger from his uncle's murderers. This was the first news Octavian received of the assassination.

---

*At birth, his father named him Gaius Octavius; historians refer to him as Octavius between birth and the year 63, when he was adopted by Julius Caesar, at which time he took the name Gaius Julius Caesar Octavianus. From that point his contemporaries knew him as Caesar; historians refer to him as Octavian (44–27BC).

He went immediately to Rome where he learned that Julius Caesar had named him successor and sole heir to his fortune. He also learned that Caesar's close friend, Marc Antony, had taken possession of Caesar's wealth and would not give it up. Marc Antony had also been made Consul and could not easily be questioned or criticized. He treated Octavian kindly but without yielding any wealth or power to the young man.

Octavian saw, as Julius Caesar had seen, that he would get nowhere without soldiers to support him. Many of Caesar's soldiers responded to his call for support. Even two legions of Marc Antony's troops sided with him. In two years, at the age of 20 and with an army to back him, Octavian forced people to vote for him as Consul. Then he made an alliance with Marc Antony and Lepidus (another powerful leader), and the Second Triumvirate was voted by the people.

All enemies of the Triumvirate were slain, in Sulla-like fashion. Among them was Cicero who was acknowledged as Rome's greatest orator and writer and who wanted to preserve the old Republic. He was assassinated by Marc Antony's soldiers. Brutus and Cassius, also supporters of the Republic, had fled to Phillipi in Macedonia and raised a powerful army there.

Octavian was now in league with Marc Antony, and they both moved men and arms to Macedonia to avenge Caesar's death. There was a great battle in Phillipi, and Brutus and Cassius were defeated. When this happened they took their own lives. Cassius killed himself with the same dagger with which he had stabbed Julius Caesar.

Now Octavian and Antony accused Lepidus of conspiring against them with Sextus, a son of Pompey. They dropped Lepidus as a member of the Triumvirate. It was resolved that Marc Antony was to be ruler of the East and Octavian ruler of the West.

By 34 BC Antony had settled in Alexandria. Captivated by Queen Cleopatra, he indulged in all manner of pleasure and high living. When Octavian heard that Antony was planning to make Alexandria the capital of the Roman world, he embarked in a fleet of swift, small boats and challenged Antony's navy at Actium. Antony's great, lumbering galleys were no match for the smaller ships and surrendered as Antony fled to take his own life. Shortly after, Queen Cleopatra killed herself.

The long struggle between the East and the West, which had begun with the battle of Marathon in 490 BC, was now completed at Actium in 31 BC, for Caesar Octavianus, the ruler of the West, became master of both East and West. He was 31 years old.

Augustus, artist unknown, Vatican Museums, 1st Century, white marble

Octavian, now the ruler of every inch of Roman territory, was given the title "Augustus" (meaning "the Honorable One"). He called himself Imperator (Commander) and did not assume that he was more. But Imperator came to mean more than just a commander of soldiers; "Emperor" came to mean the ruler of more than one country.

When Augustus returned to Rome after Actium, he allowed the Senators to think they were the rulers. Actually more and more of the direction of all affairs in Rome and the territories under her rule fell to Caesar Augustus. He managed these affairs in a peaceful way. For the first time in 200 years, the gates of the Temple of Janus were closed and peace reigned. The wealth of Rome increased as never before. Although Augustus was a man of simple tastes, the Roman public gave in to excesses of all the pleasures that money could buy.

Now "all roads led to Rome" from far more distant places than the Italian cities. Augustus did not seek to conquer new lands after establishing the boundaries of the Empire. They were natural boundaries: the Rhine and the Danube Rivers in the north, the Euphrates in the east, the Atlantic Ocean in the west and the great African desert in the south. He believed that the Empire was as large as it should be to be governed well. Its frontiers made for a peace that lasted through his lifetime as Emperor (31 BC to 14 AD, 44 years).

The boundaries of the Roman Empire were defended by the "Roman Legions," foreign soldiers who were given Roman citizenship in return for service. They were boys from Spain, Africa, Egypt, Gaul and even Germany. The Roman Legions were seldom seen in Rome because Rome was at peace.

Taxes were used to build roads, aqueducts, bridges and public buildings; the work was done by the legions stationed at the frontiers. Little towns resembling Rome sprang up from Jerusalem to Britain, each with its forum, circus, and basilica or "hall of justice." New buildings also appeared in Rome.

On the Mediterranean Sea, ships of commerce passed each other carrying people from one part of the Empire to another. The travelers were officials, architects and students on their way to Greece.

There was much traveling along the Roman roads. One might see the coach of a Roman governor, or a cohort of five hundred legionnaires marching to some station of duty and for whom all make way, or an officer leading a shackled prisoner, or a rider of the Imperial Post, or elegant ladies riding in palanquins. Wagons and caravans of camels and donkeys transported tin from Britain, spices from India, purple dye from Syria and, from Egypt—wheat, papyrus, linen, glass, embroideries.

The "Pax Romana" established by Augustus endured in spite of disturbances by barbarian tribes beyond the borders of the Empire.

To reward Octavian for having established peace in the world, the Senate wished to pay him the honors of a god. The wise Emperor, however, wanted first to find out from the Sibyl whether the world would some day see the birth of a greater man than he. Written legend has it that Augustus heard a voice that said, "A heavenly Child, the Son of the Living God, will be born of a spotless Virgin," Whereupon the Emperor erected an altar on Capitol

Roman aqueduct: Pont du Gard, France

Hill beneath which he placed the inscription, "This is the altar of the Son of the Living God."

On the 19th of August, 14 AD, Caesar Augustus, for whom this month had been named, was at his country house in Naples. He was an old man of 76 years and in miserable health. A few days before, he had attended games given in his honor. Since then his strength had steadily declined, and on this day he began to have difficulty speaking. He knew the last moments of his life were upon him. Lying upon his couch, he called for a mirror that he might see his own face. He ordered his hair to be combed. His cheeks were badly sunken and he wanted them pulled up. Then he looked at the circle of friends who were standing around him and asked, "Do you think I have acted my part well, on the stage of life? If so," and he now quoted a Greek poet, "with joy your voices raise in loud applauses to the actor's praise!"

Dismissing all except his wife Livia from the room, he turned to her with whom he had lived happily for forty years and said, "Live mindful of our union, Livia; and now farewell." With these words his spirit left his body quickly and quietly, as he had always wished it would. Soldiers carried his body to Rome, traveling only by night because of the daytime heat. The journey took several days.

His coffin, in the shape of a golden couch, was carried from his palace on the Palatine to the Forum. It was draped in purple and on top lay an image of the Emperor dressed in the robes of his office. In the procession, another image of him, cast in gold, was borne. Images of his ancestors back to Aeneas and the Goddess Venus were also carried. The Forum was crowded with people who had come to honor Augustus.

To the sound of trumpets and muffled drums, the funeral procession, followed by throngs of people, made its way slowly along the bank of the River Tiber to the Campus Martius where the pyre had been erected. Wine, oil and spices were solemnly poured upon the pyre. Then the name of the dead Caesar was called three times and, when no answer broke the silence, the pyre was lighted. The flames and smoke rose high. As they watched, many people believed they saw in the smoke the shape of an eagle carrying the spirit of the dead Augustus to heaven.

Thus ended the time in which the Roman Empire had been organized and established in peace and order, a time known as the Golden Age of Rome.

TIBERIUS CAESAR 42 BC–37 AD

Before his death Augustus had written his will, in his own handwriting on parchment, and he had given it to the Vestal Virgins to be safeguarded until after his death. Now they brought it to the Senate where it was read. In it Augustus named the man who was to be the second Emperor of the Romans: Tiberius, the son of Livia by a former marriage, for Augustus had had no son of his own.

As a boy, Tiberius had been a solemn, silent child. He had sandy hair and large, near-sighted eyes, which made it necessary for him to squint when he wanted to see something more clearly. His mother wished he wouldn't squint so much, wished he would sit up straight and close his mouth because it usually hung open in a stupid way. Yet Tiberius wasn't stupid. He was extremely intelligent. His interest in the affairs of the grownup world and his level-headedness were such that his schoolmates called him "old man."

At mealtime he would sit and listen to the talk of Augustus and Agrippa, the Emperor's son-in-law. Tiberius would imagine how goods and people were flowing toward Rome from all parts of the world. He had seen cargoes brought in on the backs of pack-horses and in barges coming up the river. It interested him to think of all these cargoes traveling from place to place as if binding together far-off countries and unknown people. When he came of age, he had many a chance to visit these far lands.

Before he was 21, Tiberius was sent as a soldier to Spain. His next assignment from the Emperor was to lead troops beyond the borders of the Empire into Armenia for the purpose of crowning a new king friendly to Rome. Upon his return, while still only 21 or 22 years old, his stepfather sent him on an even more honored assignment: to be the Governor of Gaul. As a boy, Tiberius had seen some of the strange people from the forests to the north—Gauls, dressed in their scarlet and plaid cloaks and long, peculiar trousers, and tall, blond

Soldiers of Gaul, Larousse Illustre, 1898

Germans, dressed in wolfskins—wandering through Roman streets and staring at the buildings.

When Agrippa died, Augustus felt that his daughter, Julia, should have another husband. Her two sons, Gaius and Lucius, were dear to Augustus who thought that one day Gaius would take his place. These two boys now needed a father, and Augustus selected Tiberius, on whom he depended more and more. Tiberius did not love Julia but he married her to please Augustus. Julia was not like Tiberius. She loved pleasure and flirted with the many men who swarmed in to the feasts and entertainments she provided. Tiberius found himself in a loathsome position—his wife, the daughter of the Emperor, was living a scandalous life, yet he could not bring himself to tell Augustus the truth about her. His only solution was to leave Rome and withdraw from public office.

The Island of Rhodes had always appealed to Tiberius as a place to live. There he gathered many of the teachers and scholars from both East and West. There he could read, study and live the quiet kind of life he enjoyed. He had no ambition for power and he found that life in Rhodes suited him perfectly.

When Gaius was grown, Augustus assigned him to be governor of Armenia. Tiberius visited him there. It had been twenty years since Tiberius had been sent there on a special mission. Lucius, at this time, was assigned to posts in Gaul and Spain.

In the meantime, Julia finally brought trouble to her father. She became involved in such a shocking scandal that Augustus was shamed and would see no one. He came to realize why Tiberius had left Rome. He then banished Julia from Rome and decreed a divorce between Julia and Tiberius. Augustus never saw his daughter again.

When the Emperor wrote Tiberius about what had happened, Tiberius begged Augustus not to be so harsh with Julia and expressed the wish that she should keep all the gifts he had given her. He also requested permission to return to Rome, saying that, although he did not wish to re-enter public life, he would help Gaius and Lucius prepare themselves for their great future.

Strangely, Augustus' answer was no. "Since you were so ready to desert your family, you may dismiss all anxiety concerning them." As Tiberius read these words in the Emperor's letter, he wondered when, if ever, he would see Rome again.

Whatever the Emperor's reasons might have been, Livia gave her husband no rest until he relented and sent word to Tiberius to return. So, on a day in 2 AD, when Tiberius was about 45 years old, he boarded a Roman galley and, with all his bags and boxes and rolls of books, sailed back to Rome.

Within the year that followed his return, Gaius was wounded and died in Armenia; Lucius was stricken with fever in Spain and died on his way home. Still Tiberius had no desire for public office but, because a young German chieftain on the northern border was raising an army against Rome, Augustus called upon Tiberius to go and put down the uprising.

The young German, Hermann (his Roman name was Arminius), had been a soldier of the Roman legions, as had many Germans, and he had a dream of a German Empire like unto the Roman Empire. The territory north of the River Rhine was only half-conquered by the Romans, yet they had managed the affairs of the German tribes therein. When Hermann captured all the Roman forts and outposts on the German side of the Rhine, it was feared that he might advance into Gaul which was Roman territory. Tiberius stopped him. Then Augustus and Tiberius decided not to seek further power north of the Rhine. This was a turning point in history, eventually leading to the independence of the German nation.

Augustus was now an old man and Tiberius became his constant companion for the two years before his death. Augustus adopted Tiberius as his son and heir. When the will of Caesar Augustus was read, the Senate sought to honor Tiberius Caesar as they had honored Augustus by naming the ninth month, September, for him. Tiberius cut short what he thought was a silly practice. "There are only twelve months," he remarked dryly. "What will you do when you have thirteen Caesars?"

At first Tiberius was a good ruler, although generally frowning and silent. He made laws against lavish games and spectacles. This made him unpopular, even though these laws saved money for the Roman treasury. He made just tax laws for the people in the provinces, the far off lands, and these made him popular there. He seemed more interested in the people far away and less in those close at hand. He despised the Roman populace!

Just as he thought it tomfoolery to have a month named for him, he also thought it nonsense to pretend that anyone other than he ruled Rome. He thus began to be thought of as a tyrant and lost the good will of many. He became suspicious of plots against his life and was easily influenced by Sejanus, a scheming man anxious for power, to leave Rome and live in safety near Naples while Sejanus acted as his deputy in Rome.

Sejanus then set about to accuse and put to death many who were supposedly speaking against Tiberius, even in jest. Sejanus' greed for power grew to the point of plotting against Tiberius. Tiberius became suspicious of Sejanus and finally saw to it that he was convicted of treason and put to death. By now, Tiberius' suspicions against all were aroused, and his last days were spent in acts of injustice and cruelty. Out of fear, he never returned to Rome. After 23 years as Emperor, he died in 37 AD, unloved and unmourned. He was 75 years old.

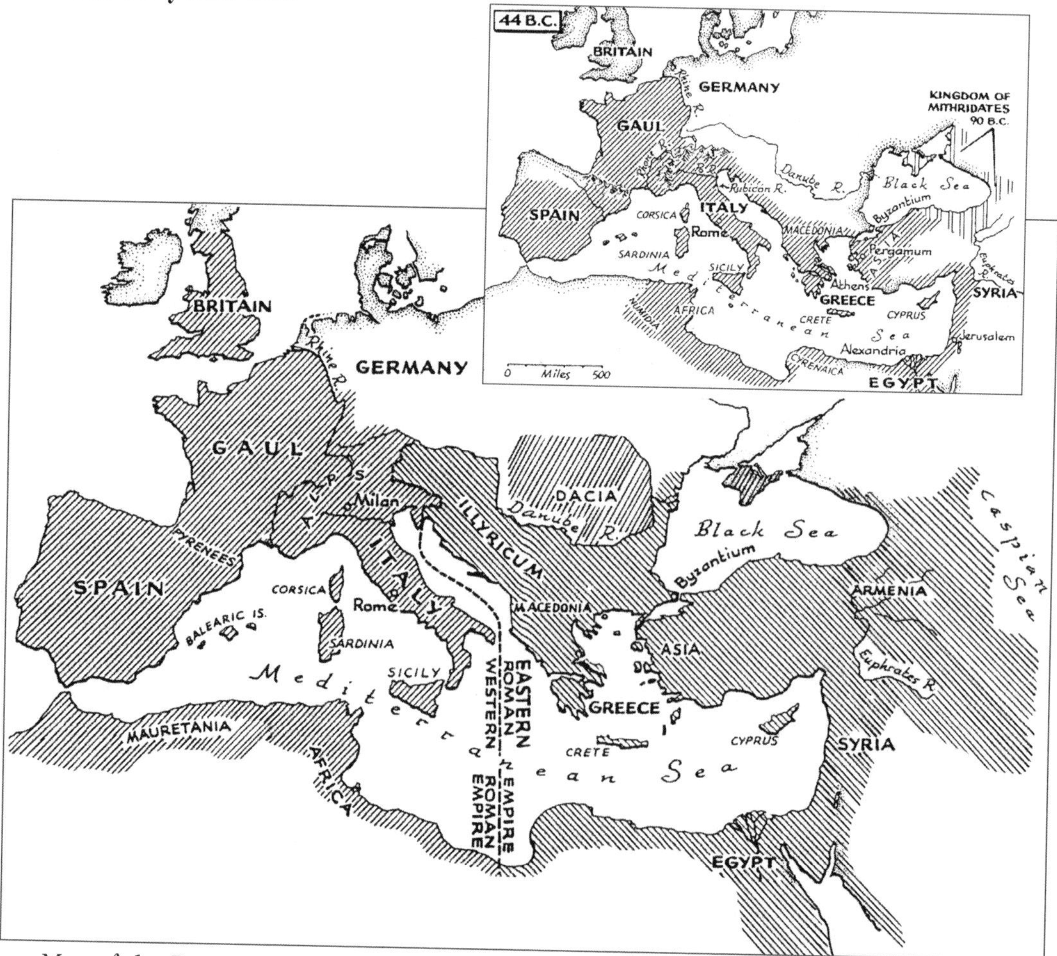

Map of the Roman Empire at its greatest extent, 117 AD. *Inset:* Roman Empire 44 BC

The Condition of the World at the Time of the Birth of Jesus

Roman power was at its height. At the pinnacle of this power was the Caesar. A popular saying was, "There is no god but Caesar." There was no true Roman religion. In the beginning, Rome had borrowed her gods from Greece, but the worship of these gods had now become so unimportant that Augustus built new temples to revive religion, but he also built a temple to "the Divine Julius" that people might worship Julius Caesar. Julius had been assassinated on suspicion that he wanted too great a power on earth, yet he was also revered as if he were a god. People had begun to look upon their Emperor as a god. Augustus enjoyed such reverence, and statues of him appeared everywhere and a temple to him was erected on Capitol Hill even before his death, after which temples were dedicated to him all over the Roman Empire.

Tiberius, Augustus' successor, was no "god." Something had changed. He did not entertain people; there were no games or combat as public spectacles. As a young man, he had taken a great interest in the actual happenings in the world around him, had been selfless toward his Emperor, had thought about life. When he was in Rhodes, he had taken a special interest in the study of the stars.

In the year 6 BC an especially brilliant star had appeared in the sky. The astronomers found that the star was actually three planets—Saturn, Jupiter and Mars—shining together in Pisces. Such a coming together of these planets is a remarkable event. They rise together in Pisces only about every 800 years. Around 800 AD, nobody noticed the stars. It was a

The Star of Bethlehem (detail), Frederic Leighton (1830–1896), oil on canvas, 1862

period called the Dark Ages. The appearance of these planets together was noted in 1604 AD and will be due again in 2408 AD. Some think this bright "star" was the one that led the Three Magi on their journey in search of the Christ Child.

A MESSIAH FORETOLD

For centuries all mythologies had dreamed of a Divine Child. He was spoken of in the temple Mysteries. Astrologers calculated His coming. The Sibyls foretold the fall of the many pagan gods. Five hundred years before Christ, Aeschylus, the Greek poet and dramatist, dared to have a character in one of his plays say that the reign of Jupiter would end, and for that he was almost put to death by the Athenians. Virgil wrote that the end of the Age of Iron had come, and a Golden Age would be ushered in by the birth of a Child, the Son of Apollo, the Sun God.

Not only in the book of Genesis in the Bible, but also in the scriptures and mystery schools of ancient India, Egypt and Greece, it was taught that God made man in his own image. In the mystery of Dionysus it was believed that the souls of men came from the smoke of his body when he was destroyed by the Titans; that when men's souls ascended to heaven to rejoin his heart, set by Athene as a sun in heaven, then Dionysus lived again.

These Greek mysteries taught that in every human being there is a spark of God. At certain periods of human history, when it is a question of saving humanity from evil, there comes a chosen one in whom that which is Godly is completely present. Such a one is called a Messiah.

STORIES OF THE LIFE OF CHRIST

Among the peoples conquered by Rome were those who were called the children of God. These were the people of Israel who were worshippers of Jehovah, the one God. They had been conquered and ruled before by nations who did not believe in Jehovah—by the Assyrians, the Persians, and now by the Romans. Through all the centuries, the Hebrews had looked forward to the coming of the Messiah, who would free them from bondage, and Whom all their prophets had foretold. So it was that people in the land of Israel, priests in the mystery schools of the East, and certain astrologers who believed in the prophecies were filled with wonder at the birth of the Christ Child.

Jehoshoua, whom we call Jesus, was the son of Miriam, whom we call Mary and who was the wife of a carpenter named Joseph. Mary of Galilee was of noble birth.

Jesus was born during the reign of Augustus Caesar when the doors of the temple of Janus were closed. Rome, the greatest power on earth, was at peace. King Herod ruled in Jerusalem for Rome. When three Kings from other eastern lands came searching for "the new King," whose birth was foretold by the star, Herod was suspicious and in fear for himself. He hid his fear and told the three Kings to find the child and let him know where they found him so that he too might go and worship Him.

After the Kings found the Child and had given him gifts of gold, frankincense and myrrh, they were warned by God in a dream that they should not return to Herod, and they went back to their own countries by another way.

Then, in a dream, an angel warned Joseph that he should take the Child and his mother to Egypt to escape from Herod. When this was accomplished and when the Eastern Kings did not return, Herod decreed that all male children two years old or younger should be slain. Many were the mothers weeping for their slain boys. "A voice was heard in Ramah, weeping and great mourning, Rachel weeping for her children; and she would not be comforted because they are not." (Jeremiah 31:15)

When Herod died, Joseph had another dream in which an angel appeared and said, "Arise and take the young Child and his mother and go into the land of Israel; for they are dead who sought the young Child's life."

When Joseph returned to Israel, he heard that Herod's son was King, and, fearing him, he took his family to Galilee, to a city called Nazareth. There he settled and took up his trade as a carpenter.

The young boy, Jesus, helped his father in carpentering, but Joseph died when Jesus was yet a young man. Joseph had brothers who would carry on his trade, so Mary gave Jesus permission to leave home and join a

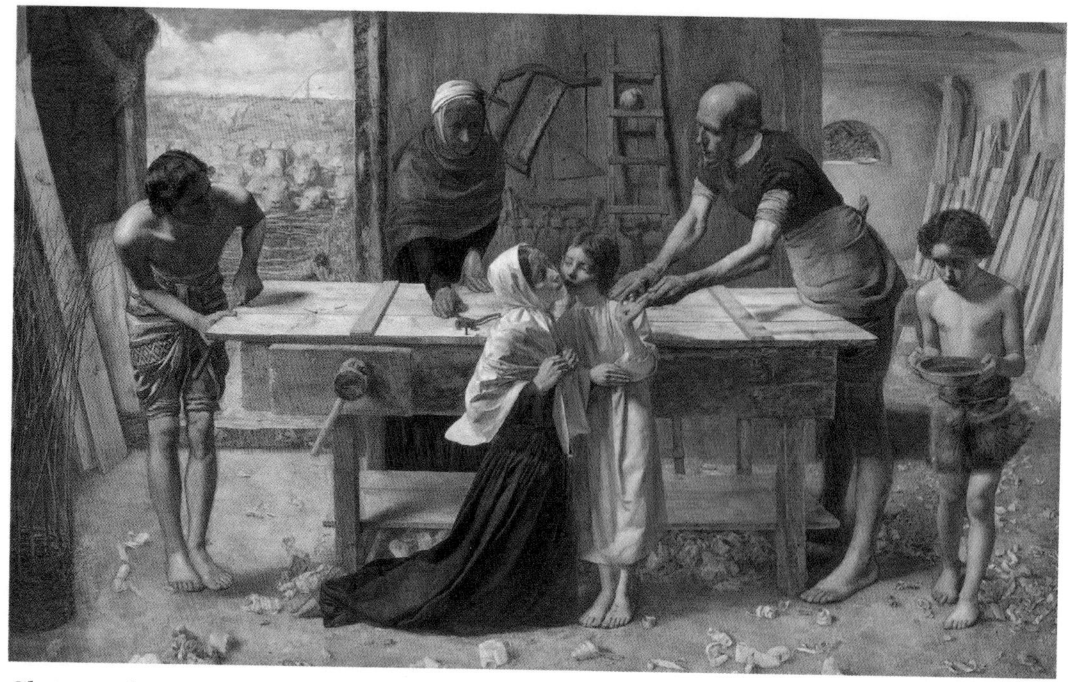

Christ in the House of His Parents (The Carpenter's Shop), John Everett Millais (1829–1896), oil on canvas Tate Gallery, London, circa 1849

brotherhood of men who lived in a remote place where they could devote their lives and their thoughts to God and to the mysteries that had come down to them from ancient times. The men of this Brotherhood were called the Essenes.

In the late 20th century, archaeologists found ancient caves near the Dead Sea in which crumbling scrolls of writings by these Essenes have been found. The scrolls were so old, so fragile, that much delicate care has been given to piecing them together so as to read new bits of the history of these times. The scrolls have revealed that a great struggle was going on between the powers of light and the powers of evil in the affairs of mankind.

Jesus of Nazareth spent several years with the Essenes. He studied the secrets of outer nature and also shut off his physical senses to meditate about mankind and its purpose in living. He also questioned himself: Why was he alive? What was he to live for?

The time came when the Head of the Order of the Essenes, said to be always one who had reached an age of 100 years, felt that Jesus showed signs of being as great as the prophets of old and that he deserved to drink from a golden chalice from which, according to the Essenes, Moses and Abraham had drunk. But no one could tell Jesus what his life was to be. He would have to discover it for himself. "Nothing from the outside; all from within." This was the very opposite of what had developed in the Roman Empire at that time. People were, more than ever before in history, ruled by laws from "outside."

At this time, a man known as John the Baptist was preaching to the crowds that gathered around him that the Messiah would soon come to drive out the Romans and re-establish the Kingdom of Israel in peace and justice, and that to prepare for his coming, people should repent of their sins. As a symbol of this inner repentance, he led many into the waters of the River Jordan and baptized them to wash away their sins. From all parts of Palestine the multitudes came to hear John, were baptized in the Jordan, and camped for weeks by the river waiting for the Messiah to appear.

It happened, then, that Jesus joined the throngs and came before John the Baptist to be baptized.

> Now when all the people were baptized, it came to pass that Jesus was also baptized; and while He prayed, the heavens were opened, and the Holy Spirit descended in a bodily form as a dove upon Him, and a voice came from Heaven, saying, "Thou art My beloved Son; in Thee I am well pleased." (Luke 3:21–22)

Then Jesus departed. John the Baptist was left full of wonder, feeling sure that he had seen the Messiah, "the joy of his days."

When these things were happening, Tiberius Caesar was 74 years old and nearing the end of his life, and Pontius Pilate was the Roman Governor of Israel.

After his baptism, Jesus was called the Christ, meaning "the anointed." This meant that Jehovah had chosen him and would be with him. Leaving the Jordan, Jesus Christ went alone into the mountains where he remained for forty days. One who has studied his life wrote that he went to a cave that the Essenes provided for their pupils who wanted to face the test of loneliness, as had the ancient Egyptians. And just as Buddha had gone by himself to meditate under the Bodhi Tree until he had found the answer to his question about God's goodness in the face of human suffering, so Christ sought to find an answer to the questions that the world put to Him. What were these questions?

Had Israel's kings and priests triumphed over the powers of evil in the world? No. Israel was dying under the Roman sword. Would the sword put an end to the reign of the sword? Should he lead his people to overturn the Roman power on earth? Or should he tell them to seek the Kingdom of God within their own souls?

At the end of forty days, Christ hungered, says the Scripture, for he had not eaten. Then there appeared before him the form of Satan, a form of the Devil, who said, "If thou art the Son of God, command this stone to become bread." And Jesus answered, "Man does not live by bread alone." (Matthew 4:4)

Then Satan led him up to the summit of a mountain from where he could see all the kingdoms of the world in one moment of time. "If thou wilt worship me," said Satan, "I will give you these glorious realms to rule."

And Jesus Christ answered, "Thou shalt worship the Lord thy God, and Him only shalt thou serve." (Matthew 4:10)

Now Satan led him to the top of the temple in Jerusalem and said, "If thou art the Son of God, cast thyself down from hence, for it is written that God's angels will guard thee and bear thee up." (Matthew 4:6)

Christ answered, "It is said that one should not make trial of the Lord God." (Matthew 4:7)

When Satan failed to tempt Jesus into doing any of these things, he vanished. Then Christ went down from the mountain to the people of Galilee and into their synagogues, and began to discuss with them the meaning of the Law given by Moses and of the sayings of the prophets of old.

Crowds began to follow him to hear his words. From among them he chose twelve men—simple men: tax collectors, fishermen and such—to be his pupils. He hoped that, with these twelve as disciples, he could begin to bring the Kingdom of Heaven to the souls of the people on earth.

Jesus had no home but traveled from place to place, always accompanied by the twelve men he had chosen as his disciples. These twelve had the idea, at first, that the Kingdom of Heaven was a Jewish government, that Christ would be crowned King, and that they would be his Ministers. Christ's words were, however: "The Kingdom of Heaven is within you," and he taught his listeners in many ways. To find the Kingdom of Heaven, he said, "Love your neighbor as yourself. Be ye perfect even as your Heavenly Father is perfect," and "All things whatsoever ye would that men should do unto you, even so do ye also unto them. For this is the law and the prophets." (Matthew 7:12)

Other words he used to instruct about the Kingdom of Heaven were given in what is commonly known as the Sermon on the Mount and recorded by Matthew, one of his disciples:

> Blessed are the poor in spirit, for theirs is the Kingdom of Heaven.
>
> Blessed are the meek, for they shall inherit the earth.
>
> Blessed are the pure of heart, for they shall see God.
>
> Blessed are the peacemakers, for they shall be called the children of God.
>
> Blessed are they who are persecuted for righteousness sake,
> for theirs is the Kingdom of Heaven. (Matthew 5:3–10)

For two years Christ went among the people, and his followers grew in number because of their longing to understand his teachings and their longing for him to free them from their oppression, and because of the miracles he performed. He taught them in parables—little stories that held in them the mysteries of the conflict between good and evil, righteousness and unrighteousness, wisdom and ignorance. One can read, in the Gospels, of the miracles by which he cured the sick, brought the dead to life, and quieted the storms of the elements. One can read many a parable.

> When Jesus entered into a boat, his disciples followed him. And behold there arose a great tempest in the sea so that the boat was covered with waves; but he was asleep. And they came to him and said, 'Save us, Lord, or we perish.' And he answered and said, 'Why are ye fearful, o ye of little faith?' Then he arose and rebuked the winds and the sea, and there was a great calm. And the men marveled, saying, 'What manner of man is this that even the winds and the sea obey him?' (Matthew 8:24–27)

In Luke's Gospel one can also find the Parable of the Sower:

Behold, the sower went forth to sow, and as he sowed, some seeds fell by the wayside, and the birds came and devoured them. And others fell upon the rocky places where they had not much earth, and straightway they sprang up because they had no deepness of earth. And when the sun was risen, they were scorched; and because they had no root, they withered away. And others fell among thorns; and the thorns grew up and choked them. And others fell upon good ground, and yielded fruit, some a hundredfold, some sixty and some thirty. He who hath ears to hear, let him hear. (Luke 8:5–8)

Then Jesus interpreted this parable to his disciples: The seeds sown by the wayside are like those who hear the word of the Kingdom and do not understand it, and the birds are the evil powers that snatch away the word of God which has been sown in their hearts. The seeds sown in rocky places are like those who hear the word of God and receive it right away with joy but have no roots in themselves. As soon as evils come against them, they stumble and give in. The seeds sown among thorns are like those who hear the word of Heaven but care more for the world and its riches which choke them, and they become unfruitful. The seeds sown in good ground are like those who hear the word of God and understand it and who, because of it, bear the fruit of goodness and mercy as gifts of heaven.

While Christ lived, many were the souls like the seeds sown in good ground, but many were like seeds sown among thorns. Many carried his word into the future, but he was hated by the Pharisees and the Sadducees, both official interpreters of Jewish Law.

In those days of Roman power, Jerusalem, the Holy City of the Jews, was surrounded by a wall on which the Roman legionnaires, spears in hand, stood watch. Here Solomon had built his temple. It had been destroyed but rebuilt more magnificently by King Herod. To visit this temple was the dream of all Jews. When Jesus was 12 years old, his parents took him to see the temple.

Drawing of a Roman legionnaire, Antoine Glédel, 2008

Entering the temple, he would have seen and admired the splendor of the marble porticoes where the Pharisees who preached the Jewish Law paraded in rich garments. He would have seen the sanctuary, or holy place, where priests, in robes of purple and deep red and decorated with gold and precious stones, sacrificed goats and bulls and sprinkled the people with blood while pronouncing blessings.

Going into the city and along its streets, Jesus undoubtedly saw beggars pale from hunger and sad-faced people who lived in their memories of past tortures and wars at the hands of the Roman conquerors. Going out the city gates he would have seen, among the dark ravines, caves from which insane men came forth shouting curses upon the living and the dead. Descending a broad stairway to the pool of Siloam, as deep as a well, he could have seen, beside the yellowish waters, the lepers, cripples, and people covered with sores. Some cried out for help; others were too stupefied by suffering to feel much need for anything. "What good is the temple? What good are the priests, the hymns, the sacrifices, if they cannot help these sorrows?" Such a question remained as an important part of Christ's teachings, and, "when the chief priests and Pharisees heard his parables, they perceived that he spake of them."

The Pharisees tried to "ensnare him in his talk." They asked him, "Is it lawful to give tribute Caesar or not?" They showed him a coin with the image of Caesar thereon. Christ said, "Render therefore unto Caesar the things that are Caesar's and unto God the things that are God's." (Matthew 22:21)

The Sadducees also came to question Jesus and to trick him with their questions. The Sadducees were a sect of upper-class Jews who accepted the five books of the Law of Moses but did not believe in the resurrection of the dead nor in the existence of angels or demons. When they asked him what he had to say about resurrection, Jesus asked them, "Have ye not read that which was spoken unto you by God, saying, I am the God of Abraham, and the God of Isaac, and the God of Jacob? God is not the God of the dead but of the living." (Matthew 22:32)

It was not until Christ spoke to the multitudes and to his disciples about the Pharisees and Sadducees, calling them hypocrites, that they began to plot against him. Some of the words he spoke about them were:

"They lay heavy burdens on men's shoulders, but they themselves will not move them with their finger." (Matthew 23:4)

"Woe unto you, scribes and Pharisees, because ye shut the Kingdom of Heaven against men!" (Matthew 23:13)

"Ye blind guides that strain out the gnat, and swallow the camel." (Matthew 23:24)

Photo from James Emery, Douglasville, US

Detail from a mural in the Church of St. Mary Magdalene. There are several variations, but the thrust of the story is this: After the Resurrection, Mary Magdalene travels to Rome and dines with Tiberius Caesar. As they eat, she tells him about Jesus, the crucifixion, and his resurrection. Incredulous, Caesar exclaims, "A man could no more rise from the dead than that egg in your hand could turn red!" The egg, miraculously, is transformed to a deep red color before his eyes in testimony to the power of God to raise Jesus from the grave.

"They say but they do not." (Matthew 23:25)

"All their works they do to be seen of men: for they make broad, their phylacteries (prayer boxes), and enlarge the borders of their garments, and love the chief place at feasts, and the chief seats in the synagogues, and the salutations in the market places, and to be called of men, Rabbi." (Luke 20:46)

And it was one of Christ's disciples, Judas Iscariot, who went to the chief priests and said, "What are ye willing to give me if I will deliver him unto you?" And they gave him thirty pieces of silver. (Matthew 26:15)

Christ was crucified, rose from the dead and ascended into Heaven, and the number of his followers increased in the Roman world. There is a "fable" that each of his disciples contributed one of the articles in what is still recited in Christian churches as the Apostles' Creed.

THE APOSTLES' CREED

I believe in God the Father Almighty,
Maker of heaven and earth;
And in Jesus Christ His only Son, our Lord,
Who was conceived by the Holy Ghost,
Born of the Virgin Mary,
Suffered under Pontius Pilate,
Was crucified, died and was buried.
He descended into hell.
The third day he rose again from the dead.
He ascended into heaven
And sitteth on the right hand of God, the Father Almighty.
From thence he shall come to judge the quick and the dead.
I believe in the Holy Ghost,
The Holy Catholic Church,
The Communion of Saints,
The forgiveness of sins,
The Resurrection of the body,
and the Life everlasting. Amen.

A Time of Change

The Romans had begun to mingle so much with other peoples of the Empire that they began to lose their identity as Romans. Egyptians, Greeks and Germans could become Roman citizens by joining the Roman legions; numerous original Romans settled and took up life in countries far from Rome. The city of Rome now became one of many Roman cities and was no longer the center of an empire.

Not only did the Romans forsake Rome, in this sense, but they also forsook the Roman gods, and the gods of other lands were brought to Rome. Temples to Isis appeared in Rome, and images of the Persian Mithra and of Cybele, the Phrygian goddess. In the streets one could meet with magicians and soothsayers from Egypt or Persia or Greece who would sell their amulets and services to anyone who would pay enough.

When Tiberius heard of the events in Palestine, he asked that Christ should be accepted as a god among the other gods, but the Senate ignored his request and pushed it aside. Much had changed since ancient times when only a few chosen men were permitted in the temple schools to undergo the training and be initiated into the mysteries of the gods. These chosen ones became the leaders of their people and had to use their wisdom selflessly for the good of all. They had the duty to teach men out of the highest wisdom. They knew that if they used their knowledge for their own selfish ends, they advanced the forces of evil in the world.

Now those holy secrets of life and of the gods were no longer in the hands of good men. They were used by many an adventurer to serve himself, by men who, untouched by true godliness, suffered inner darkness, nothingness and fear. Such a one became Emperor of Rome after Tiberius.

CALIGULA

Emperor Caligula, anonymous, Louvre Museum

As a boy, Caius had lived in the army camp where his father, Germanicus (nephew of Tiberius), was an officer. He was called Caligula, meaning "Little Boots," which he wore along with small copies of the helmet and armor of a Roman soldier. He played at being a soldier then and later.

Tiberius named Caligula as his heir. At first the young man was hailed with joy by the Roman people because he opened the arenas again and allowed the gladiatorial combats and games to be resumed for the people's entertainment. He pardoned many condemned men and spent money so lavishly that in nine months the treasury was emptied. Then the joy changed to uneasiness, for, to get more money, Caligula began to condemn rich men for crimes against him—or for no crimes—and have them put out of the way so as to take their wealth.

He then gave himself the title "Greatest and Best Caesar" and appeared in public with a golden beard fixed to his chin, holding in his hand the thunderbolt of the god Mars. At other times he appeared dressed as Venus. It was not long after that that he proclaimed he was a god; he ordered temples to be built in his honor and priests to serve his worship. He said he was the brother of Jupiter and had a bridge built from his palace on the Palatine to the temple of Jupiter on the Capitol. Crossing the bridge, he would enter Jupiter's temple, stand beside the image of Jupiter and whisper into its ear, then put his ear to Jupiter's mouth as if listening to the god's reply. Often he would shout as if in anger at Jupiter.

There was a golden image of Caligula in his own temple. Every day it was clothed in robes similar to the ones he wore on that day. His next act was to order the heads to be severed from the statues of all other gods and have models of his own head put in their places. Not only did he pose as a god on earth, but, at the full moon, he would communicate with the moon and pretend to embrace it as if he, too, were a heavenly body, a heavenly being. Yet, though a "god," he lived in such fear that at all times he surrounded himself with strong bodyguards.

Caligula never gave a thought to military matters except in pretense. Once he led some troops to the German border and sent part of them across the Rhine to pretend to attack after dark. This they did, and there was a mock battle, after which he called those who did not take part "cowards." Returning by way of the seacoast as if to attack Britain, he commanded his troops to gather shells along the beach as "the spoils of battle" to be carried in a great triumph on his return to Rome.

He loved the companionship of charioteers and horses. He provided his own favorite horse with a marble stable and an ivory manger. The horse wore scarlet wraps and a jeweled bracelet and was attended by a retinue of slaves. Caligula would invite guests to sup with him in the finely furnished stable, and the invitations were signed with the horse's name, "Incitatus." Plans were made to have the horse appointed as a consul.

In the meantime, Caligula committed ruthless crimes at will and boasted of the power he had over the lives and deaths of the Roman people. "If the Roman people had but a single neck," he proclaimed, "off comes the beautiful head whenever I say the word." Once an innocent man was condemned to death by mistake. When he heard of it, Caligula said, "It doesn't matter, for he was as guilty as others."

A Roman Emperor, depicting the assassination of Caligula and the cowering Claudius, Lawrence Alma-Tadema (1836–1912), Walters Art Museum, Baltimore, 1871

Caligula was a tall, pale man with thin legs. He had hollow eyes and a weak mouth; his upper lip hung over the lower. As a child he had had "falling sickness," probably epileptic fits. As a grown man, he could not sleep at night for more than two or three hours but would sit on his bed or walk along the palace halls, waiting for day to dawn. It was while he was so walking that one of his own bodyguards approached him and strangled him to death, only four years after he had been made Emperor.

CLAUDIUS I 44-54 AD

The uncle of Caligula had a long name: Tiberius Claudius Drusus Nero Germanicus. While Caligula was being murdered, Claudius was hiding among the curtains in a palace balcony, trembling with terror. One of the guards saw his feet beneath the curtains and pulled him out. Claudius fell on his knees, pleading for mercy; the soldier hailed him as the new Emperor and conducted him to the other guards. The next day the Senate accepted him as the fourth Emperor of Rome, although he had never held any office in government before. Claudius limped, stuttered and drooled, but none of this mattered because be was respected for his intelligence and years of study.

As it turned out, the thirteen years of his rule were of benefit to the Empire. Among his accomplishments were improvements of the port of Ostia, new buildings and aqueducts in Rome, and the conquest of Britain in an eight-year war to make it Roman. To mark this he named his son Britannicus. He also persuaded the Senate to allow Gauls to become senators.

Agrippina, the wife of Claudius, gained great power as Empress. She sat on a throne next to his. She had a son of her own and it was her will that he should be the heir to Claudius. She influenced Claudius to name him as heir instead of his own son.

"DIVINE" NERO

The way in which Nero became Emperor gives us a foreboding of what his rule (54–68 AD) was to be like. His mother, Agrippina, wished to gain all the power through him. When the astrology or stars were good for Nero, she did away with Claudius by serving him poisoned mushrooms. After his death, she commanded great public mourning and named Claudius Caesar as a new god of Rome with herself as his priestess.

During Nero's first five years as Emperor, people felt that he would be a good one. But now we know that it was because he was under a good influence, that of Seneca, his teacher, who advised him well and wrote all his speeches. Seneca had been Nero's teacher since he was a youth of 14–16 years. He knew Nero well and knew that in his nature there was a dangerous willfulness and a weakness in self-control. He knew that Nero was selfish and, at the same time, easily influenced. Seneca wanted to make sure that the influence would be for the good, at all costs. On the other hand, Agrippina set herself against Seneca, and in the struggle between Seneca and Agrippina, one dreadful event led to another.

Under Seneca's influence, Nero restrained himself, respected the Senate and tried to rule well. Agrippina did not want this, so she threatened Nero that she would bring Britannicus to power in his place. Britannicus, the son of Claudius, was then only 14 years old. Nero then acted of his own will. He served Britannicus a cup of poisoned wine. Britannicus drank it and fell dead at the Emperor's table. This was not the last of the murders wrought at Nero's will.

Nero's first wife was Octavia, the 20-year-old daughter of Claudius. But another woman, Poppaea, cast her spell on Nero. She was jealous of both Octavia and Agrippina. At her behest, Nero murdered Agrippina and divorced Octavia, who was banished and then put to death.

Seneca had said to Nero, "You have power to do many things. You know much. You can even have those persons slain whom you imagine will in any way be able to have a share in the world-order that will follow on the fall of Rome. But there is one thing beyond your power and that is those who will come after you have gone." Nero didn't seem to care. At Poppaea's instigation, in the year 65 AD, Seneca was ordered to commit suicide; this he did. In the same year, Nero killed Poppaea in a fit of rage.

Through the death of Agrippina, Nero had freed himself from her authority. He began to neglect the affairs of the Empire and to indulge himself in pleasures of his own choosing: singing and playing on the harp, acting on stage, and driving four-horse chariots.

In the year 64 AD, Rome was almost destroyed by fire. The fire was fed by persons who hurled firebrands. As the city burned, Nero called his musicians and sang of the "Fall of Troy." Rumors spread that he had ordered the flames for his own enjoyment and, although he provided shelter and food for the homeless, a murmuring against him began to grow. Public resentment led to plots against him. He went before the Senate and showed the senators the confessions of conspirators. Though hating him, the senators bowed before his authority, gave offerings of thanksgiving to the gods that Nero had been saved, and made plans to build a temple to the "Divine Nero." All who would not worship the Emperor were condemned and punished by cruel tortures and death.

At length the Senate declared Nero an enemy of the state and pronounced his death sentence. The palace guards forsook their posts. Nero fled to a friend's villa near Naples, but troops were sent after him. As the horsemen approached, he took his own life, saying, "What an artist the world is losing!"

ST. PETER AND ST. PAUL

It was during the reign of Tiberius Caesar that Christ was crucified in Judaea, a faraway province of Rome. Christ gave his life to teaching that the Kingdom of God and love were realities which every human being could bring to pass within him- or herself. The place where many criminals were crucified was called Golgotha, meaning "The Place of the Skull." Because many people felt threatened by the ideas of Jesus Christ, he was crucified there, an event that marked the coming of a new time.

Age after age, humanity had been taking ever more interest in the life of the world and, at the same time, losing its devotion to the heavenly realms. Now, at a time when the Roman power had taken possession of most of the known world, little belief remained in any other world, in any divine beings. Few believed that a human being could be a god. After the event on Golgotha, many could see the godliness in Jesus Christ, and they refused to worship the Roman Emperor as a god.

In the fourth year of the reign of Claudius Caesar, a man named Peter came to Rome. Throughout the Roman world, many men were longing for some assurance regarding life beyond death. Peter spoke of Jesus Christ as a man who had died and who had risen from the dead. Among those who heard Peter, there were many who believed him and, thereafter, ceased to worship their old gods, including the Emperor.

A legend tells us that Peter (whose other name was Simon) came to Rome because of another Simon, a sorcerer who claimed that he was a god. In Jerusalem he had come before Peter, saying, "I am the Word of God. I am the Holy Spirit. I am God whole and entire. Thou shalt soon kneel down and adore me, for I am the highest power. I can fly through the air, create new trees, change stones into bread, walk through fire without suffering harm."

When Peter exposed this Simon as a fraud, Simon went to Rome and Peter followed him. There Simon found that Nero was the god, and that no other could take his place, so Simon did the next best thing: He gained Nero's favor and served him in many ways.

Whether the legend is true or not, Peter came to Rome when the end of an ancient time was about to be accomplished. He stayed in Rome for 25 years, until the day of his death. He talked to all who would listen and led those who believed what he told them. In the New Testament we can read words like those which he must have repeated many times. In a letter to some early Christians, he said:

> "We have not followed cunningly devised fables when we made known to you the power and coming of our Lord Jesus Christ, but were eyewitnesses of his majesty. For he received from God the Father honor and glory, when there came a voice to him from the excellent glory, 'This is my beloved Son in whom I am well pleased.' And this voice which came from the heaven we heard, when we were with him in the holy mount."(2 Peter 1:16)

To these early Christians, he also wrote:

> "Honor all men. Love the brotherhood. Fear God. Honor the King." (1 Peter 2:17)
>
> "Submit yourselves to every law of man for the Lord's sake: whether it be to the King, as Supreme, or unto Governors." (1 Peter 2:13)
>
> "It is better, if the will of God be so, that ye suffer for well doing, than for evil doing." (1 Peter 3:17)

"Servants, be subject to your masters, not only to the good and gentle, but also to the froward [contrary, difficult people]. For this is thankworthy, if a man for conscience toward God endure grief, suffering wrongfully. For what glory is it if, when ye be buffeted for your faults, ye shall take it patiently? But if, when ye do well and suffer for it, ye take it patiently, this is acceptable to God." (1 Peter 2:18)

"For Christ, the just, hath suffered for the unjust, that he might bring us to God." (1 Peter 3:18)

Another who came to Rome was a Jewish tentmaker who was born Saul of Tarsus. He had been a student of the Laws of Moses and believed them with all his heart. In Palestine he had helped the high priests persecute and drive out the followers of Christ. One day he was on his way to Damascus to arrest certain Christians and bring them to trial. Suddenly "there shone round about him a light from heaven. And he fell to the earth and heard a voice saying, 'Saul, Saul, why persecutest thou me?' And he said, 'Who art thou, Lord?' And the Lord said, 'I am Jesus whom thou persecutest.'"

The Apostle Paul, attributed to Rembrandt (1606–1669), National Gallery of Art, Washington, DC, circa 1657

St. Peter in Prison (The Apostle Peter Kneeling), Rembrandt (1606–1669), Israel Museum, 1631

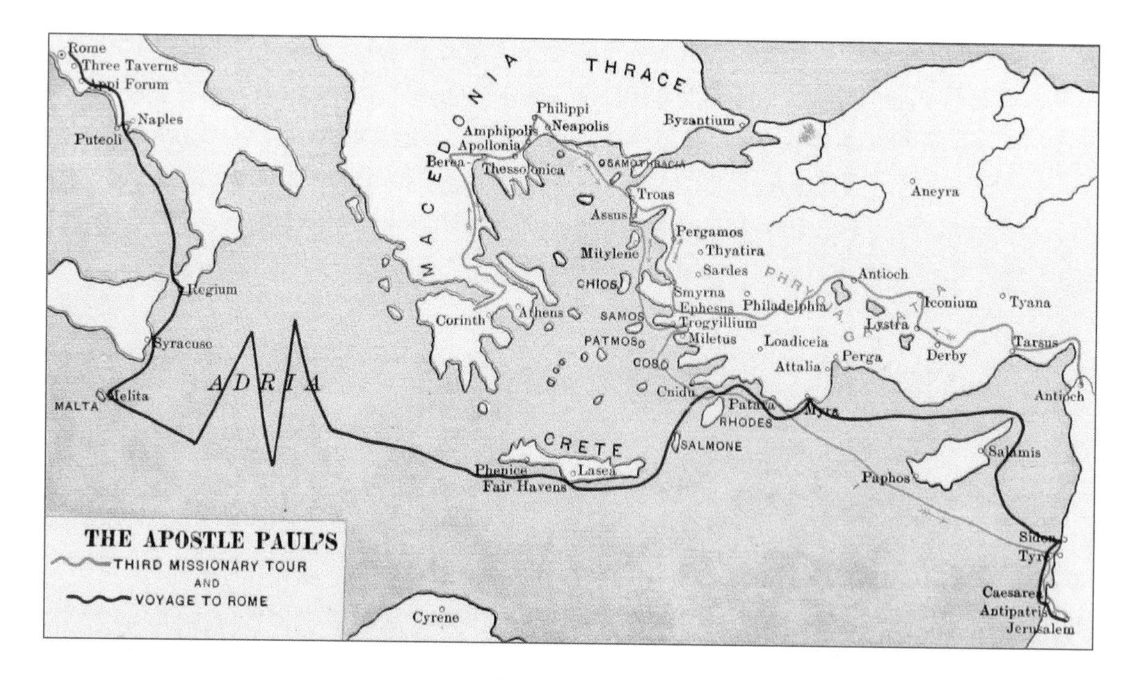

When Saul arose from the earth, his eyes were open but he could see nothing, and those who were with him had to lead him by the hand into Damascus. He remained blind for three days and neither ate nor drank. Thereafter Saul took the name Paul, meaning "small," because of his great humility. And he went among the Christians—not to arrest them but to join them.

Paul traveled throughout the Mediterranean world. He earned his living making tents and, after his day's work, he met with groups of people and spread the word that the prophecy of Isaiah had been fulfilled, that Christ, the Son of God, had come, had passed through death, and lived still.

After time spent in Athens, Corinth, and Ephesus, Paul went to Macedonia and then returned to Jerusalem. There he was thrown out of the temple by Jews who were angered by his presence. They were about to kill him when the chief Captain of the Roman forces saved him, bound him in chains, and took him to the castle of the Roman governor. There he was scourged for causing a disturbance, for all Jerusalem was in an uproar. As they bound him with thongs before striking him, he said to the centurion, "Is it lawful for you to scourge a man who is a Roman and uncondemned?" When the Jews pressed their charges against him, Paul demanded that, as a Roman citizen, he be permitted to appeal to Caesar. It was in this way that Paul came to Rome, as a prisoner, to appear before Nero.

It was 25 years after the event on Golgotha, and Nero had been reigning for two years. When Nero heard that the Jews were in dispute with Paul about some Galilean named Jesus, whom they claimed was dead and whom Paul claimed was living, Nero gave little heed and permitted Paul to go about in Rome as he wished. Paul joined Peter.

To the people who listened to Peter and Paul, and who wanted to understand their words, Christ's teachings became ever more real. Christ had said, "Come unto me, all ye that labor and are heavy laden, and I will give you rest." (Matthew 11:28) When life brought suffering, this had meaning. The suffering could be endured with peace of mind, even with happiness.

Among the early Christians were people born to suffer, the slaves. A rich Roman had hundreds of slaves, men and women or their ancestors who were the booty of the border wars. They were not even considered as human beings but were bred like cattle. Families were not allowed among the slaves. None could marry as they might have if free. Children were separated from their parents. When slaves revolted, they were lashed into obedience.

Roman officials discovered a secret society among the slaves; members of the secret society used a mysterious sign. By drawing a fish in the sand or on a wall, strangers could show each other that they were Christians and become friends. Every seventh day, the Sabbath, whole groups of slaves would disappear and meet in some obscure part of Rome to hear the words of Peter or Paul, to pray and to worship God. Heavy whippings failed to stop them. Although they continued to work faithfully for their masters, they went time and again to their Sabbath-Day meetings and returned, each time, knowing that the whip awaited them. Soon others joined the secret society—soldiers, craftsmen, and people from among the poor and lowly as well as well-to-do Romans.

The first terrible suffering of the Christians took place after the burning of Rome when Nero placed the blame for the fire on them. Thereafter, the Christians were noticed more, and it was found that they not only refused to sacrifice to the Emperor as a god, but would not take part in any holiday in honor of the old gods; they would not make bricks for a pagan temple and tried to stop the cruelty of the gladiators in their public battles. They openly prophesied that Rome would fall and that a new time would follow.

It was soon decided that Christians were criminals against the state, and, in punishment for their crimes, they were sought out and put to death.

Their punishments were many and cruel. They were set defenseless in the arenas while lions and tigers were turned loose against them. As death approached, they prayed, and thousands of Romans enjoyed the spectacle. Others were beaten to death with leaded scourges. Some were placed alive in leaden chests and thrown into the sea. Some were bound to stakes and their flesh torn from them with iron hooks. In the face of these tortures, when they were given the choice to be saved if they would return to emperor-worship, they would answer, "As long as there is breath in my nostrils, I shall not deny my God."

Seneca was one of many who were deeply impressed by these martyrs. He felt that not only do these men meet death bravely, but they even smile as if with happy hearts and they show good will toward those who have power over them.

Many people who witnessed the brutality inflicted on the Christians felt in themselves a strange, new courage which made them seek out Peter and Paul and become baptized. The meetings and the places of the meetings had to be most secret. Outside of Rome and under the surface of the earth were the burial grounds of an ancient people. Passageways connected the caverns where the dead were buried. Here in these catacombs, the Christians met to hear the story of Christ and then went forth to bring yet others back with them. Even certain high-placed Romans were joining the Christians. When Nero heard that some of his trusted officers had gone over to these Christians, he commanded that Peter and Paul be put to death.

Friends persuaded Peter to flee, but tradition tells us that, on his way out of the city, a figure of light stood before him and spoke: "If thou leavest Rome, I go there to be crucified a second time." Thereupon Peter returned to Rome and was immediately seized and taken to be crucified. He asked to be crucified upside down because he did not feel worthy to be crucified like Christ in an upright position. At the same time Paul was led to another place where he was beheaded, for he was a Roman and beheading was considered a kinder death.

NERO'S SUCCESSORS

The Emperors who followed Nero were, on the whole, men of character who worked hard to serve the Empire and the Roman citizens throughout its regions. It is interesting that among the eight emperors who succeeded Nero, not one of them was a true Roman except for one aged senator, Nerva, who ruled for only two years. Vespasian and his two sons, Titus and Domitian, were Italians. Trajan and Hadrian were Spaniards. Antoninus Pius and Marcus Aurelius were Gauls. The span of their rule was from 68–180 AD.

VESPASIAN ruled for ten years. He pulled down Nero's palace and built the Colosseum on the land where it had stood. Vespasian came from a poor family. He himself lived simply and set about ways of saving money for the State. He ruled from 68–79 AD.

The Colosseum, Lawrence Alma-Tadema (1836–1912), private collection, 1896

TITUS was Emperor for three years, 79–81 AD, and was called "the Delight and Darling of Mankind" because he sought to win the love of his subjects. Actually, as a general he had been feared for his cruelty. He destroyed Jerusalem and brought the golden vessels of the Jewish Temple to Rome. The Jews were driven out of their holy city and dispersed. There were three calamities during Titus's reign: another fire in Rome, a plague, and an eruption of Mt. Vesuvius. Titus died of a fever.

DOMITIAN reigned for 15 years (8l–96 AD). He built new and splendid buildings, increased the soldiers' pay, and took the money for it from the rich, who disliked him for it. During his time the persecution of the Christians was renewed. Domitian conquered Britain as far north as Scotland. He was assassinated. He had no son.

The old senator, NERVA, kindly and gentle, was important because he chose Trajan to succeed him. TRAJAN was the first provincial to become

Bronze statue of Emperor Nerva (96 AD–98 AD), Forum of Nerva, Rome

Statue of Trajan, London

Emperor Hadrian, anonymous, Altes Museum, Berlin

Emperor. He ruled for nineteen years, and under him the Roman Empire reached its greatest extent to include Armenia, Assyria, Mesopotamia and Media. No further conquests occurred after that.

HADRIAN, a kinsman of Trajan, carried out no more conquests during the 21 years of his rule (117–138 AD). His aim was to govern well and to civilize the peoples within the boundaries of the Roman Empire. His armies were stationed along these boundaries only to defend them. Hadrian visited every part of the Empire and established the same laws in all parts. He built a temple to Zeus in Athens and a Roman wall in northern England. He completed the Pantheon to the gods in Rome and commissioned his own tomb (now known as the Castel Sant'Angelo) on the bank of the Tiber River. He appointed Antoninus Pius as the next Emperor.

A portion of Hadrian's Wall, Milecastle, England

ANTONINUS was gentle and peace-loving, hence his surname, Pius. Peace and contentment reigned under him for 23 years. He was the first

Portrait of Antoninus Pius, artist unknown, British Museum, ca. 140 AD

to insist on the law that all are innocent until proved guilty. His nephew, Marcus Aurelius, succeeded him and was Emperor for 19 years.

MARCUS AURELIUS

Marcus Aurelius was devoted to Antoninus Pius and wanted to imitate him in all ways as a personality but, as Emperor, he could not because his reign was full of wars and other calamities. He was not a warrior at heart. He was a philosopher-king and would have been the most happy to have lived a quiet life of study and thought; but he accepted his destiny to rule on horseback at the head of his army in the midst of din and excitement. Wherever he was, he was thinking, planning and working for the good of the Empire. His greatest gift to the world was his character, which came to be known in a small volume of thoughts or "Meditations," which he wrote down in his spare moments. One such meditation is: "Waste no more time arguing about what a good man should be. Be one."

Bronze statue of Marcus Aurelius, Musei Capitolini, Rome

Invasions and attacks by the Parthians, Germans and Britons were repelled by Marcus Aurelius, and the attackers were defeated. But a plague was brought to Rome by returning soldiers. The wars and the plague used up the money in the Treasury, so the Emperor sold his own treasure to raise funds: bowls of gold, crystal vases, the gold-embroidered robes of the Empress, the crown jewels. He regarded the Christians as enemies of the Empire because they worshipped a God who had nothing to do with it, and he was merciless in his repressions and persecutions of these Christians. Yet he was good to the poor and reduced the brutality in the public gladiatorial shows as much as possible.

Marcus Aurelius was nearly 60 years old when he died in 180 AD. He had been greatly loved, but on the day of his death no one felt sad. All were sure that he had come to them from the gods and had now returned to them. So passed the last great Emperor. His son, Commodus, was weak and unworthy, a man like Nero, and he was assassinated.

THE SOLDIER EMPERORS

During the hundred years after the death of Marcus Aurelius, 29 different emperors were elected by the Praetorian guard. All but four were murdered by rivals. Commodus was murdered, Pertinax was murdered. The Praetorian guard then sold the Emperorship at auction to the highest bidder. Julianus, a former consul, bought it but reigned for only two months. SEPTIMIUS SEVERUS, an African general in command of the legions along the Danube, came to Rome, deposed Julianus, and became Emperor. He ruled without the Senate. Then his son, CARACALLA, took his place. He conferred Roman citizenship on all free men in the Empire, but he was cruel, disliked and murdered.

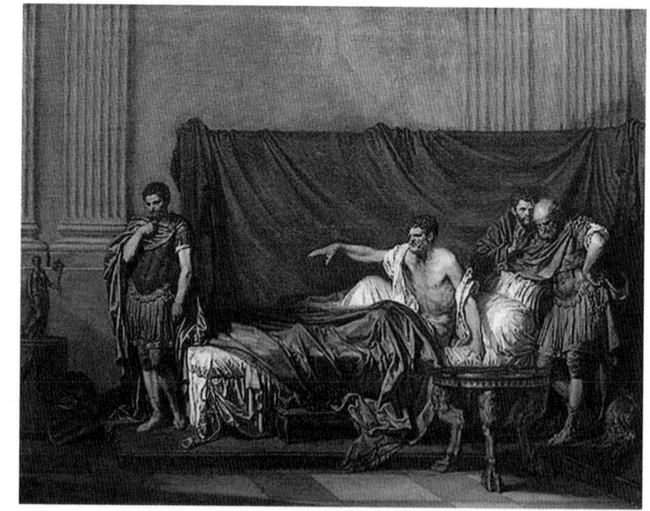

Septimius Severus and Caracalla, Jean-Baptiste Greuze (1725–1805), Louvre

After the death of Caracalla, Rome had a new ruler almost every year, and for the next fifty years there was constant civil war over the succession to the throne. Life and property were no longer safe, the army was weakened, and the German tribes to the north began to push south in search of food and lands. They overran Gaul and Spain, burning Roman cities.

In 284 AD, DIOCLETIAN, the Commander of the Praetorian Guard, was chosen Emperor. He acted like a Persian king, wearing a golden crown and golden garments and requiring people to prostrate themselves on the ground before him. He revived worship of the Emperor, and the persecutions of the Christians were worse than ever before. He abolished the Senate and ruled the Empire alone. He divided the hundred provinces into four large groups—Gaul, Italy, Illyricum (Greece) and the Orient—each called a prefecture and ruled by a Prefect directly responsible to the Emperor. Then Diocletian divided these into two parts, East and West, he to rule the East, MAXIMIAN to rule the West. Both took the title of Augustus but Diocletian held the real power. Two "Caesars" were appointed to assist the two Emperors.

In 305 AD, Diocletian abdicated and forced Maximian to do the same. The Caesars became the Emperors, and new Caesars were appointed. One of the new Emperors was named CONSTANTINIUS. He died after one year, and the army in Britain made his son, Constantine, Emperor of the West.

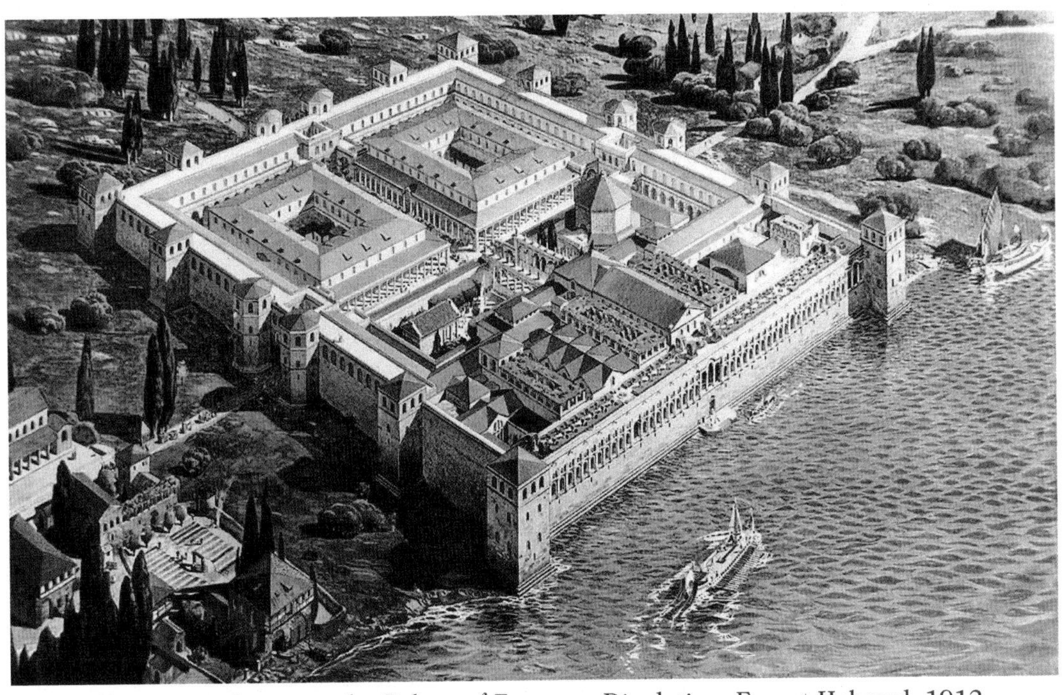

Illustration depicting the Palace of Emperor Diocletian, Ernest Hebrard, 1912

CONSTANTINE THE GREAT

Apparition of the Cross of Constantine, Jacopo Vignali, 12th century, Florence

Constantine had to overcome a rival who had been set up as Emperor by the army in Italy. Again, civil war!

Constantine's mother, Helena, was a Christian who had made a pilgrimage to the Holy Land and brought back a piece of the wood of the Cross. Constantine was not a Christian, but the story goes that, as he approached Rome with his army to drive out his rival, he saw in the sky a great, flaming cross under which he could read the words, *In hoc signo vinces,* "In this sign, you will conquer." He took this as a sign that the God of the Christians would help him in the coming battle and commanded that the sign of the Cross be placed on the shields of his soldiers. He won the battle and became sole ruler of the Empire. In 311 AD, he published an edict, the Edict of Milan, granting freedom and safety to all Christians.

For his capital he chose Byzantium, an Eastern city on the shore of the Black Sea. He changed its name to Constantinople. He had a feeling that Rome was like an old man near to death, but that the greatness of her spirit might come to life again in a new place.

The Palladium of Athena, an image of the goddess, was said to have fallen from heaven into ancient Troy. It was said that those people who possessed it and preserved it would be granted the leadership of the world, It had, in earlier times, been brought to Rome and buried in a secret place. Now Constantine took the Palladium to Constantinople to be buried in new soil. He was also said to have and to treasure some pieces of the Cross on which Christ had died. These he made into a stand for the image of the god Apollo, and he made the nails from the Cross into the rays of a crown for the head of Apollo. This statue and stand were then set over the burial spot of the Palladium. On the stand was written, "That which is active here will, like the Sun, endure for all time and will bear with it the might of its founder, Constantine, into eternity."

Constantinople was dedicated to Mary, the Mother of Christ, in 330 AD, and no pagan religion was allowed in it from then on. Constantine believed himself to be the beginner of a new era. He was baptized as a Christian on his deathbed, in 337 AD.

THE DECLINE OF ROME

Constantine's aim in moving the capital of the Roman Empire to Byzantium was to renew the greatness of Rome's spirit, but the Rome of his day was sick and dying. Even he was despotic, although more humane than others, and the democratic impulses, which for hundreds of years had guided Roman citizens, were overcome by the ancient Eastern attitude of dependence on the ruler at the peak of the pyramid.

It was no longer possible for citizens to take part in the decisions of the state. It was only from the military that new leaders arose, not as freely interested men but as men seeking power for themselves.

So great were the taxes demanded by the government that small independent farmers could not manage to survive on their farms. The rich men took over large tracts of land, and the farmers had to work the land for the landowners. Although the farm workers were not slaves, they were bound by law to the land they worked and passed with it from owner to owner as the land changed hands. They belonged to the land that their grandparents had owned and now belonged to the rich men who had acquired it. These farm workers and their descendants were called "coloni." Rome had won no new lands, hence no new slaves as captives of war. The coloni, however, were as unfree as slaves without hope of bettering themselves and their children.

Many country people, unwilling to become coloni, left the fields and turned to the city for relief. Great stretches of unworked and weed-grown fields became a common sight, so there was not enough food to feed the Roman world properly. Prices were so high in the cities, the government had to distribute free grain, wine and meat to waiting lines of the poor. Time that could have been spent in work was wasted by the cheering crowds at chariot races, bloody games and spectacles. But there was no work for the coloni in the cities because there was no money with which to pay them. The gold and silver mines of the Empire had been used up. Those who were still rich had to provide the funds for government. If a rich man became a government leader, he had to assume a financial burden, so fewer men sought these honors; many of the wealthy avoided responsibility. When money became so scarce that business transactions ended, the government had to tax people in grain and pay its soldiers with grain.

These soldiers were no longer of Roman origin but were from other lands. Rude, barbarous men had thus become the highest power in the state. The provinces felt themselves to be the equal of Rome. It was these barbarian soldiers who had fought for the right to name the emperors for so long—eighty emperors in ninety years during the age of the "soldier emperors." Through them the citizens lost their liberty.

The will of the Emperor was the law. His decrees, posted throughout the Empire, told the citizens how much they could earn as wages, how much they would pay as taxes, what kind of work they should do. No man could change his trade. Whether a butcher, a weaver, a smith, or whatever, a man had to remain at his post to supply the population. In some places, the State forced the son to follow the occupation of his father. So it came about that every man had little choice but to toil for the State and was not free to follow his own interests.

NEW CHRISTIAN LEADERS

In a realm only partially related to the Roman State, men with qualities of leadership did arise. After Constantine's Edict protecting Christians, more and more ecclesia, or churches, were established as more and more people became Christians. Men who had powers of leadership found, in the churches, encouragement and a chance to be independent. These Christian leaders were soon to become influential in the world in the same proportion as the leaders of the state became weaker. In any large city, the leading priest who became responsible for all the churches in that city was called the Bishop. He in turn could become an Archbishop when given authority over the other bishops in surrounding cities. Under the bishops were the priests and the deacons, who did not preach but who helped the priests with the practical management of the churches.

The bishops were the successors of the apostles. St. Peter was the first Bishop of Rome, and subsequent Bishops of Rome took his place and were chief priests of all the churches. When the Emperor moved his court to Constantinople, the most important man left in Rome was the Bishop of Rome. In 445 AD, a decree was issued that the Bishop of Rome was the Ruler of the worldwide Christian Church.

Now the ideal was to unite the world in a great spiritual kingdom, of which Rome was to be the earthly center, but of which Christ was to be the King and which was to last forever.

JULIAN, THE APOSTATE

Now there was a man who rose up against this development of Christianity. He did not persecute the Christians or abolish their churches, but he tried to renew something that had been great in the past, but had been almost forgotten by people in the West, and which had never been known by the barbarians in Gaul, Britain, Germany and elsewhere.

As we look back in history to ancient China, Greece, Egypt, Persia and India, we recall that, in the more distant past, human beings were guided by men who received their wisdom through initiation in the mystery schools. The wisdom of the Priest-Kings of Egypt or of the philosophers of Greece contained a knowledge of the Creation of the World and of the spirit of man. It was this wisdom of the mysteries of life that Julian wanted to re-establish among the people on earth. He did not believe that the Roman emperors were gods, but he was never sure whether or not Christ was one to further this spirit of ancient times.

He came to be called Julian the Apostate. An apostate is one who disagrees with his religion, and "Apostate" was the name given Julian by the Christians because he abandoned Christianity.

Julian was the nephew of the Emperor Constantine. Before Julian was born, those who still acted as oracles in the temples (the Sibylline Oracles), prophesied that a child would be born who would oppose Constantine. The Emperor's supporters made plans to murder this child at birth, but the plans failed. The child was born and lived, and the people who had plotted against him comforted themselves by saying, "Whatever attempts against Constantine he might make will be easily stopped and will come to nothing because we are forewarned." However, for many years they did not know what these attempts would be.

When Julian was on a military expedition in Gaul, there was a man who, one night, walked in his sleep. As the army marched by, the sleep-walking man pointed to Julian and cried, "There is the man who will re-establish the old gods and bring back their images!"

The imperial family to which Julian belonged did everything in its power to teach him Christianity, but he rebelled against it. The more he was pressed toward it, the greater was his wish to escape it. Instead, he developed a great love for the writings of the Greeks, beginning with Homer and including Pythagoras, Socrates, Plato and others. In Eleusis near Athens, Greece, there remained a mystery school of the ancient wisdom. Julian went there and became an initiate in these mysteries.

As history took its course, Julian became Emperor after Constantine's death. Then he did everything in his power to renew these mysteries and to find out if Christianity had any reality. He heard that Christ had foretold that the Temple at Jerusalem would be destroyed so that no stone of it would be left standing on another. He knew this had happened when Titus destroyed Jerusalem; but Julian wished to prove or disprove the power of Christ's

Julian the Apostate Presiding at a Conference of Sectarians, Edward Armitage (1817–1896), Walker Art Gallery, Liverpool, England, 1877

prophecy, so he set about to rebuild the Temple. He gathered many workers for the purpose, but when they approached the place to start construction, it is said that flames of fire shot out toward them, and they had to withdraw. This temple was never rebuilt.

Then Julian hoped to strengthen his purpose by going to Persia and seeking out the Persian mysteries. This coincided with a military campaign against the Persian kingdom which was, as usual, causing trouble for the Empire. But again he failed and was killed in the battle against the Persians.

Julian was the last emperor to oppose Christianity, and the Christian Church was now free to become the strongest power in the Roman world.

Thy Rome died many deaths. Her native power
By slow diseases, such as nations know
When liberty is lost, became a show
And pageantry for slaves; then came the hour
Of outward death, as when a withered flower
Falls in a tempest; o'er her lying low
The barbarous legions in restlessness flow
Rained seas of death on temple, street and tower.

– Rev. Theodore C. Williams

The Barbarians

If we were to look at a map of Europe at the time of Constantine, we would see no separate or particular countries but would find grasslands north of the Black Sea, mountains north of Greece and Italy and forests north of the Alps. These lands were inhabited by people who lived as tribes, each made up of about a hundred families, who moved from place to place in search of forage for their herds. They built no sturdy houses but lived in slight huts which were easily moved. They had little interest in farming. These people were the Goths from what is known today as Germany.

In appearance the Goths had great bodies, fierce blue eyes, long reddish or blonde hair, sometimes twisted in a knot on top of the head, and long beards. They wore tight-fitting trousers and cloaks fastened by clasps at the throat. The main tribal groups were Visigoths, Ostrogoths and Vandals.

They were used to cold and hunger, but not used to heat or thirst. They had powerful strength for fighting, but little will for daily work. Their wealth consisted of herds of cattle, horses, sheep, goats and pigs. These served as money while gold was prized as jewelry. They ate fruit, game which they hunted, and grain raised by their slaves and women. They drank mead made of fermented grain and sour milk. They loved to gamble with dice. In peacetime, the warriors became lazy and loafed—sleeping, eating and hunting—while the women did the household and field work. When a youth became a man, the tribe gave him a spear and shield in the presence of the whole tribe. It was a dishonor to lose his arms.

The warriors met in a council, or Thing. If they approved a proposal, they clashed weapons. The Head of a tribe was called a King. The warriors were not permitted to excel the King in bravery. They did not trade but plundered for their worldly goods. They wandered in search of plunder, followed by their wives and families who traveled in heavy wagons. Their fighting groups contained a hundred men from each village. When fifty villages banded together, they made an army of five thousand but each hundred fought together as a battle unit. Every man in a unit knew the others well. This made him fight fiercely.

The Romans had become soft and comfort-loving. They could not have fought off invaders because the Emperors had long since allowed Germans to settle within their frontiers, even hiring them as paid soldiers in the Roman army. Thus, Rome was defended by barbarians fighting barbarians.

Among the tribes who invaded Roman lands were the Franks from along the Rhine; the Allemani from along the Danube; the Angles, the Saxons and the Vandals from around the Baltic and North Seas; and the Goths, Visi and Ostro (meaning West and East) from the Black Sea region.

When these early invaders settled and mixed with the civilized people of the Empire, they held office, married high-born Romans, became educated and converted to Christianity. One Goth, Bishop Ulfilas, translated the New Testament into Gothic, having made up Gothic writing from the Greek and Latin alphabets. This is the earliest example of the Germanic language.

The greatest invasion of the Goths (375 AD) came in the East Empire during the reign of Valens, the Emperor of the East. The Goths had fled in fear from the swarms of horsemen, called the Huns, who came upon them

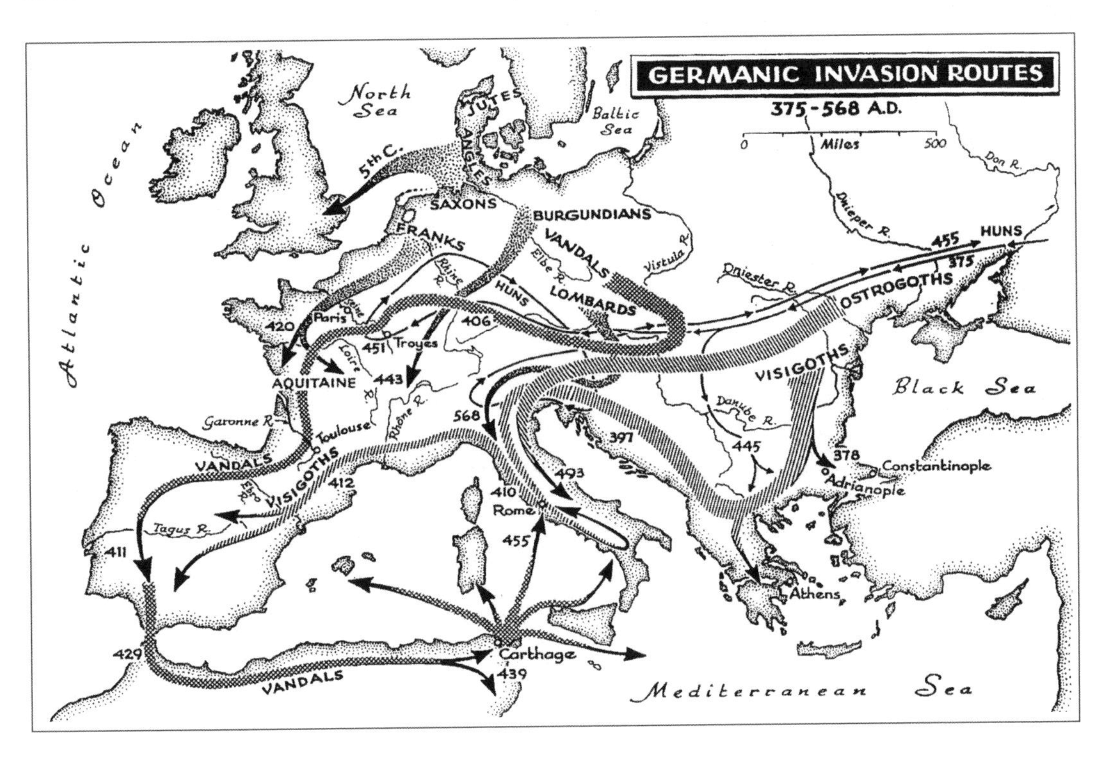

from the North and East spreading terror, for wherever the Huns passed, they left everything in ruins—merely for the pleasure of destroying—and took gold and silver, which they treasured but did not use. Attila, their great chief, boasted that grass would not grow again where his horse had passed.

The Huns were not blue-eyed, fair-skinned people, but black-eyed, yellow-skinned people, with squat bodies, bow-legs (from riding horses), flat noses, large ears and bristling hair. In habits, they were filthy and ferocious. It was not known where they came from exactly, but legend says they were born in a desert of witches and demons.

The Visigoths fled before them toward Roman territory, where they begged asylum. Valens, who succeeded Julian as Emperor of the East, allowed them refuge on the condition that they lay down their arms. This they did. Once disarmed, Roman officials took advantage of them and sold them provisions at the highest prices. Gradually the immigrants exhausted their money, then sold their slaves and even their children, until they had nothing left. They started to take by force what was refused them. They banded together, manufactured weapons and, looting and pillaging, marauded around the countryside. Valens collected his troops to fight them, but Germanic settlers of earlier times joined the Goths.

The two armies met near Adrianople. The Gothic Chief, Pritigern, first dispatched messengers of peace and kept the Roman forces waiting in the heat of an August day. They had no shelter. Thirst, hunger and fatigue exhausted them, and when exhausted thus, the Goths charged upon them and the Romans fled.

Attila, the Scourge of God, Ulpiano Checa (1860–1916), as reproduced in *Beacon Lights of History*, Volume IV by John Lord

The Emperor, deserted by his guards and wounded, had to hide in a peasant cottage, surrounded by the enemy who set it on fire. Valens burned to death.

The Goths marched in triumph to Constantinople and were defeated there by Saracen cavalry (Arabian horsemen). When the Goths moved on toward the West, there was no one to resist them. They settled in the fertile countryside as far as the borders of Italy and the Adriatic Sea.

The next Emperor of the East, Theodosius, who had Gothic blood, knew that the Goths were there to stay. He made terms with them, used their leaders to help him rule the East, and even gave his niece in marriage to one of the Germans, a Vandal named Stilicho.

This was just the beginning of an even greater migration of the barbarians into the civilized world. What they brought with them, in contrast to the Roman way of life, was a fierce quality of individuality, which bore little love for the Roman State. The Western Empire was slowly absorbed by the barbarians and broken up into small kingdoms under military leaders.

THEODOSIUS

Theodosius was a Christian. He ordered the destruction of the old Roman temples and forbade worship of the old gods. The Christian Church had gained such strength by now that it could influence the Emperor.

There was a revolt against him in Antioch, but after trying those responsible and threatening them with punishment, he pardoned them, saying, "Although exercise of justice is the most important duty of an Emperor, the granting of mercy is the greatest pleasure of a sovereign."

Yet when one of his generals was murdered by some people in Thessalonica, he lost his sense of mercy. Instead of just punishing those responsible for the crime, his mind wavered and, though the bishops begged him to pardon again, he gave in to his feelings for revenge and sent soldiers to punish the whole city. All the people were invited, in the name of Theodosius, to the circus to view certain games. When they were assembled, the soldiers massacred them, guilty and innocent, young and old alike. From 7000 to 15,000 people were killed in three hours. Theodosius knew the city well, had spent much time there, and so had a lively sense of the existence of the people he destroyed.

When the Archbishop of Milan heard of this horror, he forbade Theodosius from approaching the altar of Christ for Holy Communion until the hour Theodosius died; he could enter the Church only to pray for forgiveness.

At his death in 395 AD, Theodosius entrusted his two young sons to the Vandal, Stilicho. These sons became the emperors, Arcadius of the East and Honorius, still a boy, of the West.

"THE TWELFTH VULTURE HAS FINISHED ITS FLIGHT"

Before his death, Theodosius named Alaric (I) as tribal King of the Visigoths. Now Alaric led the Visigoths into Greece, plundered it and captured Athens. Stilicho forced Alaric back, but Alaric led the West Goths into Illyricum and was made Commander by Arcadius, the Eastern Emperor. When Honorius executed Stilicho, no one was left to oppose Alaric, who captured Rome in 410 AD.

The Sack of Rome by the Barbarians in 410, Joseph-Noël Sylvestre (1847–1926), oil on canvas, Musée Paul Valéry, 1890

The Vandals then crossed the Rhine and passed through Gaul into Spain. Three German kingdoms were set up: The Visigoths in Gaul, and the Ostrogoths in the East, and the Vandals in Spain, who acknowledged Honorius as their Emperor. The Vandals then sailed across the Straits of Gibraltar and seized the Roman province of Africa.

The Angles and Saxons, north Germanic tribes, invaded Britain. The Romans had withdrawn from Britain when Rome was being sacked by Alaric. The Western Empire had dwindled to Italy itself, and, even there, Honorius was in the hands of his Germanic commanders and officials.

Farther east, the Huns, who had forced the Visigoths across the Danube, had formed a great empire from the Black Sea to the Rhine under their King, Attila. He gained power over the Eastern Empire and made it pay him tribute. In 450 AD he led his hosts down toward Italy. The Germanic tribes rallied to assist the Western Emperor. They marched against Attila at Chalons (on the Seine) in Gaul and defeated him. Attila retreated and returned two years later to invade Italy, but he died on the way. With his death the Hunnish Empire fell to pieces and would never trouble Europe again. Now the Vandals swept up from Carthage into Sicily, invaded from the south, and captured Rome.

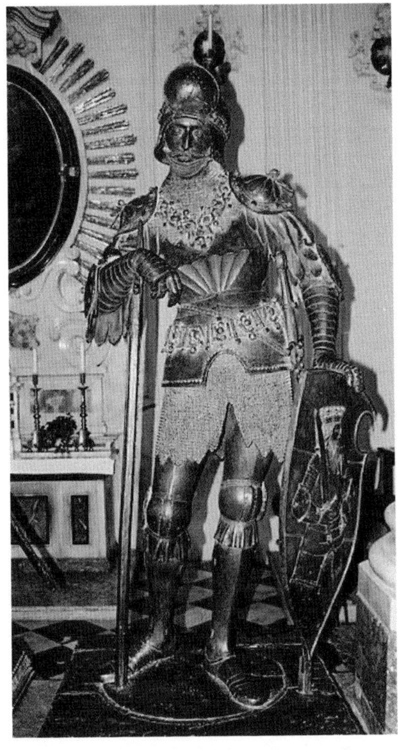
Bronze statue of Theodoric the Great, Peter Vischer the Elder at the tomb of Emperor Maximilian, Court Church, Innsbruck, Austria, 1512

From 455 AD, for the next 21 years, Rome was entirely in the hands of Germanic military leaders who made and unmade emperors as they chose. The last was Emperor Romulus Augustulus (the "little Augustus"), a young boy who bore the names of the founder of Rome and the founder of the Roman Empire. One day he was quietly set aside by Germanic soldiers, and Odoacer (one of them) was put in his place. This ended the line of emperors founded by Augustus. Odoacer sent word to the Eastern Emperor acknowledging his sovereignty and received permission to rule the West with the title "Patrician."

In 493 AD, Theodoric the Great, a Christian and King of the Ostrogoths, advanced into Italy, took the throne from Odoacer, set up an East Goth kingdom in Italy, and extended his power to Sicily, Gaul and Spain. He couldn't read but was wise and ruled well. It looked as if the Western Empire would rise again under him.

In 527 AD, Justinian I became Emperor of the East and dreamed of restoring a united empire. He succeeded in overthrowing the Vandal kingdom in Africa, passed north to Italy, and drove out the East Goths, gaining power also in Spain. Then he tried to rule the whole empire again from Constantinople. But now Italy was defenseless, and it was invaded again by the Lombards, a new, uncivilized Germanic tribe, under which it was not possible for a strong state to arise. Justinian failed to unite East and West also because of a division between the Eastern (Greek) Church and the Western (Roman) Church. So now, as there had been an Eastern and a Western Empire, there was to be a Church of the East and a Church of the West.

The Roman Empire was now nearly gone. It had existed for twelve centuries—from 753 BC, the year Romulus founded Rome, to 476 AD when Romulus Augustulus was deposed by the Germans. Augurs had declared that each of the twelve vultures seen by Romulus represented a century in the life of the city. Finally, the twelfth vulture had finished its flight.

Roman stadium built between 80–90 AD, probably a gift from the emperor Domitian, Patras, Greece

Bibliography

De Voragine, Jacobus, comp. *The Golden Legend*, 1275. English translation by William Caxton, Philadelphia: Temple Classics, 1980.

Foster, Genevieve. *Augustus Caesar's World*. San Luis Obispo, CA: Beautiful Feet Books, 1996.

Hamilton, Sir John and Dr. Harry Elmer Barnes, eds. *The Illustrated World History*. First edition, New York: Wm. H. Wise, 1935, Third edition, 1938.

Isenberg, Irwin. *Caesar*. New York: American Heritage Publishing Company, Inc., 1964.

Lang, George, trans. *The Meditations of Marcus*. The Harvard Classics, Charles W. Eliot, ed., New York: P.F. Collier & Son Corp., 1937.

MacCauley, Thomas Babbington. *Lays of Ancient Rome*. Available in eBook, Gutenberg Project, and in print, London: Forgotten Books, 2012.

Mills, Dorothy. *The Book of the Ancient Romans*. Tacoma, WA: Angelico Press, 2007.

Schuré, Édouard. *Great Initiates: A Study of the Secret History of Religion*. First published in 1889. Hudson, NY: SteinerBooks, Garber Communications, Inc., 1961.

Tappan, Eva March, ed. *Stories from the Classics: The Children's Hour, Vol. III.* Available in eBook format and in print, Glouchestershire, UK: Dodo Press, 2009.

Tappan, Eva March. *Roman History*. New York: Houghton Mifflin Company, 1910.

Virgil. *The Aeneid*. Robert Fagels, trans., New York: Penguin Classics, 2008.

———. *The Aeneid of Virgil Translated into English Verse.* Theodore C. Williams, trans., First edition, New York: Houghton Mifflin Company, 1908, Third edition, 1938.

Williams, Henry Smith, et al., eds. *Historians' History of the World: A Comprehensive Narrative of the Rise and Development of Nations as Recorded by over Two Thousand of the Great Writers of All Ages.* New York: Encyclopedia Britannica, 1904.

Made in the USA
Charleston, SC
30 August 2016